Learning
Power
in Practice

RUTH DEAKIN CRICK

Learning
Power
in Practice

A Guide for Teachers

P·C·P

Paul Chapman
Publishing

KH

Paul Chapman Publishing
A SAGE Publications Company
1 Oliver's Yard
55 City Road
London EC1Y 1SP

SAGE Publications Inc.
2455 Teller Road
Thousand Oaks, California 91320

SAGE Publications India Pvt Ltd
B-42, Panchsheel Enclave
Post Box 4109
New Delhi 110 017

Library of Congress Control Number: 2005910371

A catalogue record for this book is available
from the British Library

ISBN-10 1-4129-2219-4   ISBN-13 978-1-4129-2219-7
ISBN-10 1-4129-2220-8   ISBN-13 978-1-4129-2220-3 (pbk)

Typeset by C&M Digitals (P) Ltd., Chennai, India
Printed on paper from sustainable resources
Printed in Great Britain by The Cromwell Press, Trowbridge, Wiltshire

11/17/06

for Jackie Carpenter
who showed her students the sky

Contents

Foreword

The publication of *Learning Power in Practice* represents an important stage in the development of the Effective Lifelong Learning Inventory (ELLI) project. ELLI has been 'work in progress' within the University of Bristol's Graduate School of Education for the past five years. Like most of the projects funded by the Lifelong Learning Foundation (LLF), it combines a robust scientific strand with a strongly practical orientation, the aim being to develop a range of tools for tracking, evaluating and recording people's development as real-life learners.

The success of a project of this type depends to a significant degree on the quality and strength of its intellectual and methodological foundations. The ELLI project was particularly fortunate to have been guided in its early stages by Guy Claxton (Professor of the Learning Sciences) and Patricia Broadfoot (Professor of Education) at the University of Bristol, now Vice Chancellor of the University of Gloucestershire. Within this creative framework, Dr Ruth Deakin Crick has been able to give full rein to her own intellectual and research talents. Work to reinforce and extend ELLI's original foundations is continuing under Dr Deakin Crick's direction within the Graduate School of Education at Bristol.

For the Foundation, ELLI's 'cradle-to-grave' perspective has a particular significance. LLF understands 'lifelong learning' to be just that – **a coherent, inter-linked process of cumulative learning through life**. Not only does this approach set LLF apart from those who see lifelong learning as little more than a 'make-over' of conventional adult and continuing education, it also paves the way for an ongoing development process through which the sinews and energy of learning can be identified, encouraged and tracked. ELLI's importance lies precisely in the extent to which it identifies seven dimensions of 'learning power' and provides scales to assess these. In this sense it represents an important contribution to the relatively neglected field of assessment **FOR** (as opposed to **OF**) learning.

Dr Deakin Crick's book meets 'head on' the second challenge set by LLF – that the outcomes of the research should make an impact in real life. Aimed at leading-edge teaching practitioners working at all stages and levels of the learning process, the book introduces – in graphic and accessible terms – ways in which the ELLI 'dimensions' can be nurtured and developed. In the process, it also makes a useful contribution towards creating a language for understanding the importance of learning itself.

In commending this book to teachers and learners alike, the Trustees of the Foundation believe it offers a timely and practical contribution to the aim of enabling our education system to meet the challenges of learning in the twenty-first century.

Colin George OBE
Chairman, The Lifelong Learning Foundation

Acknowledgements

The first people I would like to say a big 'thank you' to are Professors Patricia Broadfoot and Guy Claxton for the original and powerful inspiration of the ELLI project.

Secondly, the project owes a debt of gratitude to the research team in year three when we researched the factors that contribute to learning power in the classroom. This team included Dr Marilyn Tew, Emma Randall, Helen Jelfs, Gary Prosser and Dr Susannah Temple. We were also joined by Dr Barbara McCombs from University of Denver who brought her invaluable expertise in learner-centred practices to the team and Alice Hadden, James Park and Harriet Goodman from Antidote, an organisation working with schools to support the development of emotionally literate learning environments.

Thirdly, there are too many to name them all, but the teachers and students who have collaborated in this project have made a vital contribution to our learning – without them we would not be here. Some of them have played such a key role in our work that I want to name their schools, colleges and universities:

- St Mary Redcliffe and Temple School, Bristol.
- Speedwell School, Bristol.
- Westbury Park Primary School, Bristol.
- Ashton Gate Primary School, Bristol.
- Christchurch Primary School, Wiltshire.
- Stoke Bishop Primary School, Bristol.
- Summerhill Junior School, Bristol.
- Millfield School, Somerset.
- University of Glasgow
- St Bartholomew's School, Berkshire.
- St John's School and Community College, Wiltshire.
- Kolej Yayasan, UEM, Malaysia.
- Worle Community School, North Somerset

Two of these practitioners must be mentioned in person: David Millington and Marcelo Staricoff, who have developed the ideas and practice of learning power as far as anyone, in their classrooms at Westbury Park Primary School, and who provide a precious window onto their work in Chapters 6 and 7.

The Lifelong Learning Foundation continues its partnership with the University of Bristol Graduate School of Education and the ELLI Research and Development Team in ViTaL Partnerships. Together these organisations sustain the programmes of research, development and enterprise through which ELLI is reaching out to learners across the world. We are grateful for all the invaluable support and advice given to the project by their leaders and directors.

Finally, I would like to express my gratitude to my close team: Guoxing Yu and Elspeth Samuel, for being such cheerful, knowing and dedicated co-researchers and supporters; Tim Small, whose writing and attention to textual detail are almost as strong as his friendship; and Sue Woodhead, whose indefatigable organisation, help and good company have kept me going through the challenges and delights of this interesting journey!

Ruth Deakin Crick
The Graduate School of Education
Berkeley Square
Bristol

The ELLI story

This book is a product of several years of professional learning involving researchers, teachers and students in an exciting and often challenging journey.

The idea for the ELLI research project came out of a creative dialogue between Professors Patricia Broadfoot and Guy Claxton and the trustees of the Lifelong Learning Foundation. This led to the first ELLI research project in which we developed the first version of the ELLI Learning Power Profiles and worked with teachers and students to see how this form of assessment data might be used diagnostically and formatively to support learning. The very first draft of the Learning Power Profiles came from work at Christchurch Primary School in Bradford-on-Avon, Wiltshire, where teachers had been working with Guy Claxton on devising practical ways of developing students' learning power.

The second phase of the research project, again funded by the Lifelong Learning Foundation, was an exploration of how learning power relates to other vital elements of learning – teachers' learner-centred practices, the school's emotional climate, school leadership, and student achievement. We also developed materials for the classroom and the 'online' Learning Profiles.

At this point, the Lifelong Learning Foundation created a charitable company to explore how ELLI could be developed and distributed more widely. A market feasibility exercise confirmed that it was something of educational and commercial importance and of significant interest to schools. Training materials were produced and ELLI 'the product' became available more widely.

Since then, a vibrant development and research programme has emerged supported by ViTaL Partnerships. Through 'R&D' (research and development) projects, each specially designed to research local conditions, creative partnerships were made with over eighty-five leading practitioners in five secondary schools and about thirty in seven primary schools. The programme was extended to Foundation Stage, a secure unit for young offenders, a school in Scotland for young people with social, emotional and behavioural difficulties and a training programme for NEET (not in employment, education or training) learners across the South West of England. Projects began and are also flourishing as far afield as Madrid and Malaysia. Many imaginative strategies for increasing learning power have been devised and trialled by these creative practitioners, many of whom have provided material and ideas for this book.

Working in these different settings and cultures has helped us to understand more about what ELLI can do and how we can get the best from it: what are the obstacles and opportunities in different ages and phases and with students having different advantages, needs and difficulties? We have been able to gauge the impact of ELLI on learner and teacher development, progression from primary to secondary school and links between personal, social and academic development. An important theme has been the relationship between learning power and curriculum content, design, sequencing and assessment for learning. School leaders have been quick to see the potential of learning power data for diagnostic and self-evaluation purposes, especially relating to the five outcomes of 'Every Child Matters'. We are also exploring the links between learning power and enterprise, learning power and mental health and learning power and the 'Opening Minds' Curriculum developed by the RSA (Royal Society for the Encouragement of Arts, Manufactures & Commerce).

Learning Power Profiles have now been developed and trialled with over 10,000 learners from the age of seven through to students in higher education, and adults. The project continues to grow, more rapidly than we could have imagined, working away at the interface of research, practice, policy and enterprise. We hope that you will be inspired by what you find in these pages and decide to play a part in the ELLI story as it unfolds.

IMPORTANT CONTACTS

If you are interested in learning more about the ELLI Research, becoming involved in its development programme or using ELLI in your setting you can use one of the links below to find information and contact details you need:

The ELLI Research Programme is based at the Centre for Narratives and Transformative Learning at the University of Bristol, 35 Berkeley Square, Bristol BS8 1 JA. www.bris.ac.uk/educ/enterprise/elli

The Lifelong Learning Foundation supports the ELLI programme and has a website where you can learn more about its work: www.lifelonglearnresearch.co.uk. It also manages the ELLI online resources and tools that are available for schools and other professionals through education consultancies. More details can be found at www.ellionline.co.uk.

ViTaL Partnerships is a charitable company that works in partnership with the Lifelong Learning Foundation and the University of Bristol to support research and development projects concerned with learner centred practices with practitioners in schools and beyond. It works to build links and stimulate dialogue between the worlds of research, policy, practice and enterprise. See more at www.vitalpartnerships.org.uk.

At www.VitalEd.net you will find a virtual meeting place for values and learning which offers

- a virtual networking environment
- a rich and growing resource bank to used and add to, including ELLI materials.

About the Authors

Ruth Deakin Crick is a Senior Research Fellow at the University of Bristol, and Director of the ELLI Research Programme. She began her career as a teacher of music and PE and progressed into school leadership as a head teacher of a community-based independent school. She worked extensively in education policy on behalf of third-sector alternative and independent schools.

Following academic training in social science, education and theology, all at the University of Bristol, Ruth began a research career in school-based professional learning around the themes of values, citizenship and learning power. She went on to develop the ELLI research project, which identified characteristics of effective lifelong learners and how teachers and schools can nurture students as learners, rather than simply examination fodder. She has worked on a number of systematic reviews of evidence for education policy and practice and is committed to working at this complex interface.

David Millington is currently a Year 5 teacher and Advanced Skills Teacher (AST) at Westbury Park Primary School in Bristol and is in his seventh year of teaching. Since his first introduction to ELLI three years ago, he has spent considerable time developing a classroom practice which builds upon the seven dimensions and helps children to become better lifelong learners. David's belief that children need a very clear understanding of what it means to be an effective learner has led to the introduction of the dimensions to his class through animal metaphor. This has in turn helped him to focus on the dimensions as a model for teaching. David has shared his teaching practice with a number of schools in Bristol, Gloucestershire, Essex and Dudley through workshops, in-service education and training (INSET) and invites to the school. David has recently featured in a set of learning and teaching continuing professional development (CPD) materials, 'Excellence and Enjoyment in the Primary Years', produced by the Primary National Strategy.

Tim Small is a former secondary head, now Director of *aHead-Space*, a support service for leaders in education. He works in over twenty schools a year across the south of England, coaching learning and leadership skills in schools in challenging circumstances and reviewing head teachers' performance with governors. He co-ordinates the ELLI Research and Development (R&D) team, specialising in the secondary phase, which takes him as far afield as Madrid and Malaysia. Working closely with schools, he creates and runs R&D projects, each 'custom designed' with its own research questions, to learn how ELLI is best deployed and to trace its effects on policy, practice, learning and achievement, in each setting. Tim has written pamphlets interpreting recent research into the impact of Citizenship Education, for practitioners and teacher educators, on behalf of the University of Bristol Graduate School of Education. Most recently, he has created the 'Courage to Be …' project for ViTal Partnerships.

Marcelo Staricoff is Deputy Headteacher at St. Bartholomew's CE Primary School in Brighton, and was previously teaching at Westbury Park Primary School in Bristol, where he led the Thinking Skills and G&T Strand of the School's Beacon Project. As Bristol LEA's Thinking Skills Consultant and Lead Teacher for G&T in the North West Bristol Cluster, he regularly hosted teachers in his classroom, who were interested in how to deliver a thinking skills and ELLI enriched curriculum. Marcelo regularly leads INSET days, runs workshops and speaks at local and national conferences.

Marcelo is a member of NAGTY's G&T Think Tank and of their Primary Expert Advisory Group. He is also a member of SAPERE's National Committee and of Brighton and Hove's Creativity Steering Group. With Westbury Park Headteacher, Alan Rees, he has written a thinking skills book entitled *Start Thinking*, published in November 2005 by Imaginative Minds. Marcelo has also published many articles in educational journals describing how a thinking skills and philosophical approach to the curriculum can induce in children a very deep and lifelong love of learning.

How to use this book

This book is written for teachers. It outlines the basic ideas and concepts of learning power as they have developed through research and it is full of practical applications of those ideas for the classroom. The examples of student learning profiles are taken directly from statistical evidence and the stories are fictitious but based on real-life experience. Chapters 4 and 5 are also based on qualitative research evidence while Chapters 6, 7 and 8 are taken from real-life examples of ways in which teachers – in action research and in their regular teaching – have given the ideas legs and let them walk right through their classrooms. The final two chapters are at the edge of our research evidence and application – and are currently the subject of research and development.

Some of the chapters, particularly Chapters 1–3, should be read through carefully, until the ideas are familiar. The classroom-based sections have been designed so that you can adapt the practices to your own situation and in some cases reproduce diagrams and checklists for use in school.

At the end of most chapters is a recommended book, website or article for further reading which builds on the ideas of that chapter.

The bibliography at the back includes a range of targeted resources – academic and professional – which will 'fill out' some of the gaps and the broad ideas of the book. If you are studying or engaging in your own research and development project around these ideas, then this bibliography may be a good starting point.

Learning power: what is it?

This chapter introduces the idea of learning power. It is worth reading this chapter carefully, because it underpins all the ideas about learning power in the rest of the book.

It explains:

- what we know about learning power
- how we can recognise learning power in action
- how learning power is part of a complex ecology of learning
- the seven dimensions of learning power that emerged from research.

INTRODUCTION

The term learning power[1] has become a popular one in schools in the last few years. Understanding what learning power is and how it relates to learning to learn, learning styles, assessment for learning and attainment is essential for anyone wanting to develop learning power in themselves or in their students. This chapter will explain what learning power is and what it is not, based on what we know about it so far from research evidence.

Learning power is something that people recognise intuitively, but it is difficult to explain and understand. This is partly because we have lost the language to describe learning well and partly because it is not something that can be touched, felt, seen or heard!

Learning power is invisible, rather like a form of energy, and this makes it more difficult to understand than something concrete or material. In fact we *can* be specific about particular dimensions of learning power, but these are presumed to be evidence of the *presence* of learning power in a person, rather than learning power *itself*. When we see light in a light bulb, we know electricity is present – we don't see the electricity itself. Learning power is similar.

In this chapter we will first explore why learning power matters and where it fits in the 'ecology of learning'.[2] Secondly we will explore what it actually is and finally we will look at the dimensions of learning power that have emerged from the research.

LEARNING AS AN ECOLOGY

Learning is not a simple thing. There are many factors that influence learning that are both inside and outside the learner as a person. For example the quality of relationships in the classroom has a profound impact on learning – trust and acceptance foster learning, whereas fear and boredom inhibit learning. How a learner feels about herself, her aspirations and hopes as well as physical comfort and levels of worry all have an effect on the quality of learning.

Climate for learning

Creating a climate for learning in the classroom means making sure that every activity, relationship and process supports the development of students' learning power

Equally, the climate of the classroom affects how learners can learn – assessment strategies in particular have an impact. For example, we know that formal testing used for grading students actually has a negative impact on learning. It influences what students think and feel about themselves as learners, how they perceive their capacity to learn and their energy for learning.[3] Yet some assessment strategies are prescribed by government, and therefore, indirectly, government policy too, is part of this complex ecology. As in a garden, the ecology needs to be optimal for growing particular types of plants. The right sort of temperature, moisture and nutrients really matter. In developing learning power we need to be able to provide the optimal ecology. Some of the key ingredients which will be touched upon throughout this book include relationships, reflection, self-awareness, motivation, dialogue, trust and challenge, time and space.

LEARNING POWER AT THE HEART OF THE ECOLOGY OF THE CLASSROOM

In a garden the whole purpose of creating an optimal ecology is to release the energy for plants to grow and thrive. In the learning classroom and school, the whole purpose of attending to the ecology of learning is to release the energy for learners to learn and change over time. That is in essence what learning power is: the life energy which is present in all human beings that leads to human growth, development and fulfilment over time. It is this life energy that is behind all human cultural, scientific and humanitarian achievements.

Back in the classroom, however, this core energy for learning is still critically important for those cultural, scientific and humanitarian achievements that make up the fabric of everyday life in school. How we can engage and harness that energy in young learners is the focus of this book.

It is sometimes the case that we get the balance wrong. It is as if what matters most is what teachers do, or the content of the curriculum, rather than learners and learning. Classrooms are still too often dominated by a focus on assessment and testing to see if standards are improving. This has actually detracted from student learning, although 'assessment for learning' strategies are beginning to redress that balance.

Perhaps a more systemic, and therefore more pernicious, lack of balance has been a focus on attainment and raising standards *at the expense of* personal development. That is not to say that the attainment of knowledge, skills and understanding is not important – it is a central purpose of schooling to which we all aspire. However, its twin purpose is personal development and preparation for adult life, including active citizenship and enterprise. This aspect of schooling, although enshrined in the preamble to legislation and in the inspection frameworks, has had far less sustained attention in research, policy and practice. As we will see throughout this book, the development of learning power is a highly personal process which sits at the heart of both attainment and preparation for adult life. It could also be a key to greater achievement by all students.

WHAT WE DO IS WHAT WE TEACH

When we teach, two important things happen, whether we like it or not. We teach the *content* of what is to be learned and we teach young people to *love* or to *hate* that learning. In other words we teach the knowledge, skills and understanding that are usually the prescribed focus of the curriculum *and, at the same time*, we teach students to form particular values and attitudes towards learning in school. The way we teach, what we do, how we are as people in the classroom and our own attitudes to learning all help to form in our students particular values, attitudes and dispositions towards themselves and learning, of which we are often unaware. Of course, these are sometimes negative towards school learning.

The forming of values, attitudes and dispositions is a central part of personal development. Personal development is an important part of the purpose of education and it includes the spiritual, moral, social and cultural development of students, the development of the dispositions and attitudes and values for citizenship, for enterprise and for the realisation of a person's full potential as a human being in the community.

The development of knowledge, skills, understanding *and* personal development always happen together. It is a profound mistake to treat them as though they are separate processes. No teacher is only a teacher of a subject – all teachers model and impart values, attitudes and beliefs through their relationships and through all they do. The person of the teacher as well as their professional 'know how' in the classroom both have an impact. A teacher's authenticity, integrity and orientation to learning and learners all influence the learning ecology, as well as the sorts of learning and teaching strategies he employs. The personal development of the teacher is as important, therefore, as the personal development of the learner.

Values: what really matters around here.

Attitudes: clusters of thoughts, feelings and beliefs about people, ideas and things.

Disposition: a tendency to behave in a certain way.

BECOMING LEARNER CENTRED

Being 'knowledge centred' leads to a learning climate where transmission of knowledge, skills and understanding becomes the most important value, and learners and teachers are judged by how well they impart or acquire that knowledge. Being 'child centred' leads to a learning climate where the child's experience is most important and learners and teachers are judged by how relevant the learning processes and outcomes are for the child. While both of these are necessary, focusing on one at the expense of the other is unhelpful. Being learner centred means that we recognise the importance of both the child *and* the knowledge, but the focus is on the *child as a learner* and the *process of learning*. When we integrate personal development and attainment we begin to harness learning power and we become 'learner centred' in our approach rather than 'knowledge centred' or 'child centred'.

When we focus attention on the learner and learning and we combine this with what we know about teaching, school and classroom organisation that best promote the highest levels of motivation and achievement for all students, then we are being learner centred, according to research from McCombs in the USA (McCombs and Whisler, 1997).

Ecology for learning

An ecology for learning is a micro-climate where learners and learning are at the heart of all that happens. Teachers seek to create the best possible conditions for learning and growth.

Creating the optimum ecology for learning is a question of values. A value can be understood as 'what really matters around here' because that is what will actually shape practice. If it is not clear what really matters, or if what really matters to policy-makers is different to what really matters to teachers or learners, then the ecology suffers.

Learner centredness also relates to the beliefs, characteristics, dispositions, and practices of teachers – practices primarily created by the teacher. According to McCombs, when teachers derive their practices from a learner-centred perspective, they:

- include learners in decisions about how and what they learn and how that learning is assessed
- value each learner's unique perspective
- respect and accommodate individual differences in learners' backgrounds, interests, abilities, and experiences
- treat learners as co-creators and partners in the teaching and learning process.

The personal qualities and skills of teachers really matter. It is as much about *who we are* and *how* we teach as *what* we teach.

THE DOUBLE HELIX OF LEARNING

A metaphor for learning power that some people find helpful is the double helix, at the heart of DNA, and therefore of life. A double helix has two strands which run parallel to each other and never meet, but are always held together.

Teaching for learning has two strands which always run together (represented in Figure 1.1). One of the strands is personal development and the

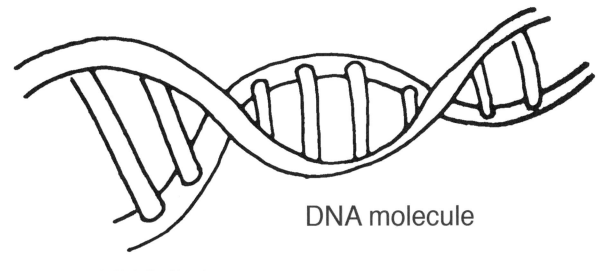

DNA molecule

Figure 1.1 The double helix of learning

other strand is the knowledge, skills and understanding that we are attending to. The question is, what is it that holds these two strands together? We suggest that learning power is the energy that runs through the middle of the double helix of learning. The seven dimensions of learning power are what hold the two strands together as well keeping them distinct from each other.

LEARNING POWER: A DEFINITION

Learning power is a complex term, and one that does not lend itself to easy definitions. One way of explaining learning power is as:

> *A form of consciousness characterised by particular dispositions, values and attitudes, expressed through the story of our lives and through the relationships and connections we make with other people and our world.*

To put it another way, learning power seems to be a form of awareness about oneself as a learner. It can be recognised in particular behaviours, beliefs and feelings about oneself and about learning. It finds expression in particular relationships, where trust, affirmation and challenge are present and it is 'storied' in the memories people bring to their learning and in their future hopes and aspirations.

It is a 'way of being' in the world, an orientation towards changing and learning over time, towards engaging with life and relationships in our personal lives and social and political communities. It is an essential element of learning throughout the lifespan, and it is a quality of *all* human beings, although the degree to which we are aware of our own learning power may vary significantly from person to person and in different contexts.

Key ideas

Learning power:

- is a form of consciousness in all human beings
- exists within and between people
- runs through people's stories
- is about thinking, feeling, wanting and doing
- can be recognised in seven dimensions.

Some young people exhibit substantial learning power outside of school, for instance in:

- text messaging
- using the internet
- crime
- fashion
- music
- sport

but these youngsters may have switched off from school and rarely utilise those same capabilities in the classroom.

Other young people may be high achievers in school, but actually not be aware of how they learn or their own learning power. Such youngsters may often be quite fragile and isolated learners, dependent on their teachers to provide them with the information they need, suffering crises of confidence after leaving school. Typically, these learners are predicted to get high grades in GCSEs or 'A' levels, but when they move on to adult learning contexts they really struggle.

Learning power is relevant to human growth and development in any context, not just schools. The notion of positive personal change over time is at the heart of much psychotherapy theory. Learning, adapting, changing and growing are central to successful enterprise and important for success in any profession. No one who has been in close contact with a tiny baby can doubt that the learning power that we are all endowed with – becoming aware of ourselves as learners, and taking responsibility for our learning and growth over time – is a profoundly important theme for all human beings.

Failing to learn or learning to fail?

Ben's small class of 'A' level biology students were all set to get A grades. Some of them had applied to study medicine at a university which had a problem-based approach to learning, in which they would first encounter real patients and their stories.

These students' learning profiles suggested that they were diligent and bright, but fragile, dependent and isolated learners. They discussed this with Ben and began to develop a language for learning. They realised that they needed to move away from depending on Ben to give them the information they needed to pass the exams and to take responsibility for their own learning journey.

Meanwhile, Ben began to give them the experience of what it feels like to fail, by setting problems which were too difficult or which had many possible answers. They began to develop resilience and team work, and their self-esteem began to be derived from their capacity to learn, rather than simply 'getting it right'.

THE SEVEN DIMENSIONS OF LEARNING POWER

The research evidence from the ELLI project suggests that there are seven dimensions of learning power that we can recognise and use as a framework for learning and assessment in many different contexts. These dimensions are *not just* about thinking, *not just* about feeling and *not just* about doing. They include all of these.

They are not the same as learning styles – or learning preferences. They go deeper than this and are qualities of human beings that form the necessary conditions for human growth and development.

They are important for all sorts of learning, both in school and out of school, for personal learning, growth and change, for healthy relationships and for the management and manipulation of knowledge and information for life in the twenty-first century. They are also highly relevant to citizenship in a healthy democracy.

The dimensions were derived from research into nearly 6,000 learners.[4] While it is not the purpose of this book to go into the research evidence in any detail, some background about where these ideas have come from may be helpful. In the original research project that identified these seven dimensions, we included all that we knew, from existing research and from practice, that contributed to our knowledge of learning and of learning to learn. This included concepts such as:

- how learners attribute their success in learning
- learners' sense of self-esteem as learners
- important relationships for learning
- learning cultures
- feelings about learning
- learning in the classroom
- learning identity and story
- learning strategies, skills and dispositions.

The statistical processes applied to the data enabled us to distinguish some strong, recurring themes which we then identified as the seven dimensions of learning power.

Learning power is about how learners perceive themselves as learners, rather than how they are seen by others, or how particular external criteria are applied to learners' behaviour. In this sense, learning power is deeply *personal*, though, as we shall see, it is not *private*. What really matters in learning power is how the learner becomes aware of herself as a learner over time and how she can apply that awareness to life and learning.

INTRODUCING THE SEVEN DIMENSIONS OF LEARNING POWER

Table 1.1 introduces each of the seven dimensions of learning power with a brief explanation of what it means and the sorts of statements that might be thought, said or felt by someone who is strong in that dimension.

Table 1.1 The seven dimensions of learning power.

Dimensions of learning power	What this dimension means	What I think and feel and do in this dimension
Changing and Learning	A sense of changing and growing as a learner	• I know that learning is learnable • I know that my mind can get bigger and stronger just as my body can • I feel good about my capacity to learn • I expect to change as time goes by • I celebrate my learning
Critical Curiosity	An inclination to ask questions, get below the surface of things and come to my own conclusions	• I want to delve deeper and to find out what is going on • I don't accept things at face value • I want to know how, why, what and where • I don't accept information without questioning it for myself • I enjoy finding things out
Meaning Making	Making learning personally meaningful by making connections between what is learned and what is already known	• I like to fit new bits of information together with things I already know • I like to make connections between subjects • I love learning about what really matters to me • I draw on my own story in my learning as well as the stories of my community • I learn at home, in my community and at school
Creativity	Risk taking, playfulness, lateral thinking and using imagination and intuition in learning	• I like to play with ideas and possibilities • I trust my intuition and follow my hunches • I use my imagination in learning • I like to be challenged and stretched
Learning Relationships	The ability to learn with and from other people and to learn on my own	• I like sharing my thoughts and ideas with people • I like learning on my own as well • I learn from adults and people at home • I like learning with and from other people • I know how to help others learn

Table 1.1	(Continued)	

Dimensions of learning power	What this dimension means	What I think and feel and do in this dimension
Strategic Awareness	Being aware and actively managing my own learning feelings, processes and strategies	• I know how I learn • I can manage my feelings of learning • I plan my learning carefully • I think about thinking and learning • I am aware of myself as a learner – I know what I like and dislike • I can estimate how long tasks will take
Resilience	The tenacity to persist in the face of confusion, not knowing and failure	• I know that making mistakes is a natural part of learning • I am not afraid of having a go • I tend to keep going at a task until it is completed • I don't fall apart when I fail • I keep going at my own pace – I know I will get there in the end • I know that struggling is an important part of learning

These dimensions of learning power are introduced as positive dimensions that support learning. In fact the research suggests that each of these learning power dimensions has an opposite. We call these the *emergent* pole which tends to be positive for learning and the *contrast* pole which tends to inhibit learning. Each pole sits at the opposite ends of a spectrum. For example, '*changing and learning*' is an emergent pole of this dimension and '*being stuck and static*' is the contrast pole. Where learners are on the spectrum of changing and learning depends on how 'much' they see themselves as changing and learning at any one time and in any one place.

REFLECTION: LEARNING POWER DIMENSIONS IN MORE DEPTH

These descriptions of the learning power dimensions will give you more detail. They are carefully worded by researchers to be as faithful as possible to the ideas that emerged from the data. Read them slowly and mull them over. The contrast pole for each dimension is also included here.

Changing and Learning

Effective learners know that learning itself is learnable. They believe that, through effort, their minds can get bigger and stronger, just as their bodies can and they have energy to learn. They see learning as a lifelong process and gain pleasure and self-esteem from expanding their ability to learn. Having to try is experienced positively: it's when you are trying that your 'learning muscles' are being exercised. Changing and learning includes a sense of getting better at learning over time and of growing and changing and adapting as a learner in the whole of life. There is a sense of history, hope and aspiration.

... and at the opposite end of the spectrum:

> ***Being static or stuck:*** *less effective learners tend to believe that learning power is fixed and therefore experience difficulty negatively, as revealing their limitations. They are less likely to see challenging situations as opportunities to become a better learner. Their feeling of self-efficacy is weak.*

● Critical curiosity

Effective learners have the energy and desire to find things out. They like to get below the surface of things and try to find out what is going on. They value 'getting at the truth' and are more likely to adopt 'deep' rather than 'surface' learning strategies. They are less likely to accept what they are told uncritically, enjoy asking questions and are more willing to reveal their questions and uncertainties in public. They like to come to their own conclusions about things and are inclined to see knowledge, at least in part, as a product of human inquiry. They take ownership of their own learning and enjoy a challenge.

...and at the opposite end of the spectrum:

> ***Passivity:*** *passive learners are more likely to accept what they are told uncritically and to believe that 'received wisdom' is necessarily true. They are less thoughtful and less likely to engage spontaneously in active speculation and exploratory discussion.*

● Meaning Making

Effective learners are on the lookout for links between what they are learning and what they already know. They get pleasure from seeing how things 'fit together'. They like it when they can make sense of new things in terms of their own experience and when they can see how learning relates to their own concerns. Their questions reflect this orientation towards coherence. They are interested in the big picture and how the new learning fits within it. They learn well because their learning really matters and makes sense to them.

... and at the opposite end of the spectrum:

> ***Fragmentation:*** *less effective learners are more likely to approach learning situations piecemeal and to respond to them on their own individual merits. They keep information stored in separate silos in their brains. They may be more interested in knowing the criteria for successful performance than in looking for joined-up meanings and associations.*

● Creativity

Effective learners are able to look at things in different ways and to imagine new possibilities. They enjoy lateral thinking, playing with ideas and taking different perspectives, even when they don't quite know where their trains of thought are leading. They are more receptive to hunches and inklings that bubble up into their minds and make more use of imagination, visual imagery and pictures and diagrams in their learning. They understand that learning often needs playfulness as well as purposeful, systematic thinking.

...and at the opposite end of the spectrum:

> **Rule-boundedness:** *less effective learners tend to be unimaginative. They prefer clear-cut information and tried-and-tested ways of approaching things and they feel safer when they know how they are meant to proceed. They function well in routine problem solving with clear-cut answers, but are more at sea when originality is required.*

Learning relationships – interdependence

Effective learners are good at managing the balance between being sociable and being private in their learning. They are not completely independent, nor are they dependent. They like to learn with and from others and to share their difficulties, when it is appropriate. They acknowledge that there are important other people in their lives who help them learn, though they may vary in who those people are, e.g. family, friends or teachers. They know the value of learning by watching and emulating other people, including their peers. They make use of others as resources, as partners and as sources of emotional support. They also know that effective learning may also require times of studying, enquiring and even 'dreaming' on their own.

... and at the opposite end of the spectrum:

> **Isolation or dependence:** *less effective learners are more likely to be stuck either in their over-dependency on others for reassurance or guidance, or in their lack of engagement with other people.*

Strategic Awareness

More effective learners know more about their own learning. They are interested in becoming more knowledgeable and more aware of themselves as learners. They like trying out different approaches to learning to see what happens. They are more reflective and better at self-evaluation. They are better at judging how much time, or what resources, a learning task will require. They are more able to talk about learning and about themselves as learners. They know how to repair their own emotional mood when they get frustrated or disappointed. They like being given responsibility for planning and organising their own learning.

... and at the opposite end of the spectrum:

> **Behaving like a robot:** *less effective learners are less self-aware and are more likely to confuse self-awareness with self-consciousness. They are less likely to be able to explain the reasons for the ways they choose to go about things. They don't tend to reflect on their own processes and experiences in such a way as to 'name them' and learn from them. They might plunge into a task with little planning or forethought.*

⬤ Resilience

Effective learners like a challenge and are willing to 'give it a go' even when the outcome and the way to proceed are uncertain. They accept that learning is sometimes hard for everyone and are not frightened of finding things difficult. They have a high level of 'stickability' and can readily overcome feelings of frustration and impatience. They are able to 'hang in' with learning even though they may, for a while, feel confused or even anxious. They don't mind making mistakes every so often and can learn from them.

... and at the opposite end of the spectrum:

Resilience

Encouraging resilience means helping learners to get better at all of the other learning power dimensions.

- Helping them to see that they can change and grow and be curious, creative and make meaning.
- Supporting their strategic awareness and developing learning relationships.

Dependence and fragility: *dependent and fragile learners more easily go to pieces when they get stuck or make mistakes. They are risk averse. Their ability to persevere is weak and they seek and prefer less challenging situations. They are dependent upon other people and external structures for their learning and for their sense of self-esteem. They are passive receivers of knowledge, rather than active agents of their own learning, constructing meaning from their experience.*

The research showed that in the first six dimensions the positive poles were the emergent ones and the contrast poles were negative. However, this was the other way round in the seventh dimension. The emergent pole was dependence and fragility and this was shown to be the opposite and counterbalance of the others. From the data, therefore, we can tell that people who have high levels of dependence and fragility tend to report lower levels of the other dimensions. So someone who is a **fragile** and **dependent** learner tends also to be **passive**, **static**, **rule-bound** and **fragmented** in their thinking. They may be either **dependent** in their learning relationships or **isolated**, and generally they **lack strategic awareness**.

When we work with these dimensions in the classroom and elsewhere we focus on the positive and name resilience as the seventh dimension. Resilience itself needs a focus. When we are encouraging resilience in learners we are encouraging them to be resilient in building themselves up on all the other dimensions.

⬤ MORE ABOUT THE LEARNING POWER DIMENSIONS

All of the learning power dimensions are related to each other. They should be treated as all part of the same thing. What is important is a learner's profile on all of these dimensions as a whole.

Learning power is not the same as attainment although there is generally a positive relationship between the two. An important distinction is that someone can succeed well in school but still be a poor learner. In our research we have found learners who are high achievers – but are also very fragile and dependent. They have typically been successful in learning where they are provided with all the data they need, which they can process easily. They have not met very much failure or learned how to make mistakes. Sometimes when these learners find themselves in situations where the answers are not obvious, or where they are required to think for themselves for the first time, they fall apart.

Their self-esteem as learners is derived from the external successes rather than from an internal confidence in their own learning power.

WHAT WE KNOW SO FAR ABOUT HOW LEARNING POWER OPERATES

There are many other aspects of learning power that we can identify from our research. Here are a few examples:

- Girls tend to have higher levels of creativity and learning relationships than boys, who in turn tend to have higher levels of resilience and strategic awareness.

  You may find girls are less likely to keep trying and are more inclined towards tasks requiring communication and imagination whereas boys are more likely to be 'up front' with what they want and to figure out more how to get their needs met, even in negative ways!

- Schools and classrooms vary in the amount of learning power reported by students.

  Learning power for students depends a lot on the quality of relationships in the classroom, the climate of the school and the teacher's learner-centred practices. These vary from classroom to classroom and school to school. This is where school self-evaluation and improvement really counts.

- Students tend to report significantly less learning power as they get older – with the greatest decline occurring in the early years of secondary school (see Chapter 8).

  The sobering facts seem to be that the average learning power score for students in Key Stage 4 is significantly lower than for those in Key Stage 3 and this is lower than for those in Key Stage 2. Something about how we are organising schooling and learning does not seem to be producing more effective lifelong learners as students go through school. Although the onset of adolescence may be part of the explanation, it does not seem likely to account for this significant reduction in learning power over the five compulsory years of secondary education. This could be a major design fault in the curriculum.

- Different ethnic and religious groups report different levels of learning – some communities are more oriented towards learning relationships than others.

  Where students belong to families within strong communities and values then they report themselves to have more positive learning relationships. Students' cultures and values are important learning tools – don't make them leave them at the door of the classroom.

- We suspect, too, that individuals will tend to have a basically stable shape to their learning profile, but that its strength may vary according to what they are doing and where they are at the time of assessment.

  For example, if Daniel loves science and his science teacher, but hates art and dislikes his art teacher, then he will probably report lower levels of learning power in art.

- Some dimensions of learning power can predict attainment.

  The more learning power students report, the more likely they are to be higher attainers, to like their teachers and to feel emotionally 'safe' in class. Furthermore, high scores in changing and learning and meaning making actually predict attainment.

 Creativity is negatively associated with attainment in maths, English and science in the National Curriculum.

The same research showed that higher levels of creativity actually predict lower attainment by National Curriculum measures. Another design fault, it seems, in our national assessment framework.

In the next chapter we will meet some individuals and explore their learning power profiles. Meanwhile, research into learning power continues and includes researchers, teachers and students themselves. What we describe here is just the beginning of a learning journey.

Summary

In this chapter we have:

- introduced the idea of learning power and made use of the metaphor of the 'double helix of learning'
- identified learning power as a 'form of consciousness' in all human beings, recognised in particular values, attitudes and dispositions
- found that attending to learning power in schools 're-balances' the tension between academic attainment and personal development and enables us to create a learner-centred school climate
- explored seven dimensions of learning power that emerged from the research, describing them in some detail as well as the relationships between them
- understood that learning power is not a single entity, but more like a form of human energy that manifests in different ways, at different times and in different contexts.

These concepts are fundamental to an understanding of the rest of the book because the success of any application of these ideas is in direct proportion to how well they are 'owned' and 'internalised' by teachers and learners. Some of the most powerful and creative applications of these ideas have arisen where learners and their teachers actually take ownership of them and apply them creatively to their own situations.

NOTES AND FURTHER READING

1. Before the ELLI project began Guy Claxton extensively developed the ideas around learning power for schools. For further reading around these ideas, see:

Claxton, G. (2002) *Building Learning Power: Helping Young People Become Better Learners*. Bristol: TLO.

And also:

McCombs, B. and Whisler, J. S. (1997) *The Learner Centered Classroom and School: Strategies for Increasing Student Motivation and Achievement*. San Francisco, CA: Jossey Bass.

2. For a more academic read about the 'ecology of learning', see a paper reporting on the ELLI project written by Deakin Crick, McCombs *et al.* (2006), referenced in the bibliography at the back of the book.

3. For more on this, see:

Harlen, W. and Deakin Crick, R. (2003b) 'Testing and Motivation for Learning', *Assessment for Education*, 10(2), 169–208.

Harlen, W. and Deakin Crick, R. (2003a) 'A systematic review of the impact of summative assessment and testing on pupils' motivation for learning', in *Research Evidence in Education Library*. London: Evidence for Policy and Practice Information and Co-ordinating Centre, Department for Education and Skills.

Assessment Reform Group (2002) *Testing, Motivation and Learning*. Cambridge: Assessment Reform Group.

4. Deakin Crick, R., Broadfoot, P. and Claxton, G. (2004) 'Developing an Effective Lifelong Learning Inventory: The ELLI Project', *Assessment for Education*, 11(3), 247–72.

Chapter 2

The stories of three learners

In this chapter we meet Emma, Sam and Habib, three young learners at different stages of their school lives. We will be following their stories and joining them on their learning journeys throughout the rest of the book.

Emma, Sam and Habib are representative of the kinds of learners we find in every school. They will help us to see how:

- students' life stories are important in shaping their learning power
- learning power does not necessarily manifest itself in obvious ways
- assessing students' learning power is a means of supporting them in taking responsibility for their own learning.

We have become acquainted with the idea of learning power and its seven dimensions. We now have a language to describe the quality of a person's engagement with his own learning. Next we shall explore three different stories, firstly from the perspective of the teachers. Then we shall learn a little more about Emma, Sam and Habib and their families, getting a glimpse of the person behind the image each presents to the world. We will begin to see how their attitudes and dispositions towards learning have been formed over time and are shaped by the relationships and communities that they find themselves in.

They have been chosen because they are typical examples of the students encountered in the research. They are representative of ordinary youngsters in our schools, rather than being particularly capable, disaffected or challenged. See if you recognise them!

EMMA, SAM AND HABIB: THE SCHOOLS' STORIES

Emma: her Tutor's report in November of Year 10

Emma is generally a delight to teach. She is quiet, pleasant, friendly and co-operative and no trouble whatsoever. She follows instructions to the best of her ability and is helpful and obedient in class. Her punctuality and uniform are excellent. She has a close circle of friends who keep themselves to themselves and stay out of mischief. There have just been three occasions of unexplained absence so far this year, when she says she has lost her notes from home. Her teachers say that she sometimes has difficulty keeping up with the pace of the work and she could improve her attention span when it comes to writing. She could also contribute a little more to whole-class discussions. As long as she continues to try hard, asks for help when she needs it and makes the effort to complete her class work and hand her homework in on time, she should be able to achieve respectable grades in her GCSEs.

Predicted grade range: A* A B C D E F G U

Target grade range: A* A B C D E F G U

Sam: his Tutor's initial feedback to parents in October of Year 7

Sam seems to have settled in happily to secondary school life. He joins in well with class discussions, puts his hand up to offer ideas and asks questions of his own, even though these are sometimes a little off the point. He sometimes distracts the class with a related story of what happened over the weekend, rather than sticking to the point of a discussion. He works well with others and often concentrates well on his own, too, especially when he is interested in the topic. He must be careful to avoid getting into trouble with his teachers for chatting too much with his friends in class. He says he likes maths and languages, where the work is clearly structured, but occasionally misbehaves in RE, drama and technology, where he is given more freedom. He could do with help to pack his bag the night before coming to school, so that he has the equipment he needs for every lesson. (Please come into school when you can, to collect Sam's mobile phone from reception – he should leave it at home or keep it switched off!)

Average SAT score (Year 6): **4.5**

Average target minimum level: **5.1**

Average current Performance: **3.9**

● Habib: his Teacher's report in March of Year 5

Habib is very good at joining in with class discussions – he always has something to say for himself. He gets very involved in his learning and sometimes resents being interrupted when it is time to move on to another topic. He is quite difficult to help, as he often thinks he 'knows best' and wants to do things his way. There is not always time to go into the questions he asks. He is very persistent and is trying hard to keep his promise to be polite at all times. He sometimes mentions the advice he gets at home and it might be worth meeting again to discuss the support you are giving him, to make sure we avoid confusing him. He still has difficulty meeting his literacy targets, especially spelling. This is a high priority in the build-up to his SATs next year. Perhaps you could help by testing him at home every night, rather than once a week as you do already. It would be great if Habib could just 'do as he is told' sometimes, without arguing about it.

Target minimum levels:

Reading: 5 a b c 4 a b c 3 a b c 2 a b c 1 a b c W

Writing: 5 a b c 4 a b c 3 a b c 2 a b c 1 a b c W

Maths: 5 a b c 4 a b c 3 a b c 2 a b c 1 a b c W

Science: 5 a b c 4 a b c 3 a b c 2 a b c 1 a b c W

● LEARNING POWER – A MISSING LINK

All of these students present different challenges to their teachers. Neither Emma nor Sam are fulfilling their potential, and while Habib is doing pretty well he is not always easy to have around.

> Learning power may help to identify the causes of underachievement.
>
> Identifying underachievement in schools is one thing – identifying the causes of underachievement and addressing them, is more of a challenge.

All the schools undertake assessment practices which predict how well their students should be doing in the light of their prior attainment and cognitive ability – and Emma and Sam are both known to be underachieving. The problem is that these assessments are not specific enough to enable teachers to diagnose the causes of that underachievement or to find ways of helping. Nor do they assess how effective these students are at the business of learning itself.

While Emma is learning in the structured environment of the GCSE year, she will probably be fine. However, what will happen to her when she encounters other sorts of learning demands such as those which will be required of her when she enters the world of work? And to what extent are her personal life aspirations being shaped by her current underachievement?

For Sam, there are indications already that he is beginning to switch off from some of the curriculum. How can the school help him to remain motivated and engaged with his learning rather than become a chronic underachiever?

Habib's teacher is already getting fed up with the challenge he presents, having plenty to do to keep the class on track for their SATs next year. For how long is Habib going to keep his confident, out-going nature at school if his slightly eccentric but effective approach to learning is not recognised and supported?

LEARNING POWER AND THE LEARNER'S STORY

So far we have understood something about learning power as revealed in a particular moment in time: how it is now. However, a person's learning profile is shaped by her story and the ways in which she has made sense of her world over her life span so far. It will also influence her hopes and aspirations for the future. How Emma might tell her own story may also be very different from how Emma's teacher or mum might tell it, but it will be Emma's perceptions, values and meanings which will be most powerful in shaping Emma's learning identity.

In the next part of this section we hear a bit more about Emma's, Sam's and Habib's stories, so as to understand them and their learning power profiles a little better as we go on through this book.

Emma's story

Emma is fifteen. She would describe herself as being quite a 'Daddy's girl' when she was little. She looked up to her father, who was in the forces, and missed him badly when he went away with his regiment. Until she was eight her mum made sure that she was always neatly turned out in her school uniform, with her hair tidy and face washed.

In her primary school, Emma was a quiet pupil who seemed attentive because she watched her teacher, but she would often be daydreaming rather than listening. When her class were given homework, she would usually ask her older sister for help. She enjoyed the classroom rules and routines and was chosen to water the pot plants every day. Her teacher once asked her why she always did this in the same order, thinking that there was some 'method in it', but Emma was unable to explain why this was.

Emma enjoyed secondary school at first, with all the different lessons and teachers and the organisation of the school day, with bells every forty minutes. She and her two closest friends soon found 'safe places' to meet and talk at lunchtime and eat their packed lunches. When she was asked if she could say why a lesson or a subject was important, she would say 'because it will help me to get good marks in the exams' or, later, 'to help me get a good job'. She did not tend to make connections between the learning in one lesson and another, or see any relevance in them to her life out of school, which consisted mainly of television, pop-idols, clothes and make-up.

The first time she had ever got into trouble was in Year 9 when she was caught smoking – something she and her friends had started doing just before Christmas, in the same toilet every break-time. In class, she was happy enough when asked to copy information from the board into her exercise book, which she did with neat precision, but usually only half-finishing by the time the bell went. She thought about other things while she did this and did not concern herself with the information left behind on the board that she had not had time to write down.

After taking the SATs, towards the end of Year 9, she began to lose interest and found herself mostly waiting for the bell to end lessons. She knew that her attitude, attendance and punctuality were always reported to be excellent until she got to Year 10, when she started skipping lessons that bored her. Although she had achieved a mixture of level 5s and 6s in her Year 9 SATs, she was failing to achieve much in her GCSE courses and was found a college placement in Year 11, preparing for a vocational course in Health and Social Care.

Sam's story

Sam was always a very happy child. He is the youngest of three brothers, with quite a big gap between him and the other two. He was the apple of his parents' eyes and adored by everyone around him.

His early childhood was spent happily with his brothers, whom he admired a lot. He learned by imitating them, and joining in with their games. Of course he could never quite keep up with them, and they would often help him out with tasks that were a little way beyond his reach. When the boys had new computer games, Sam simply copied what his brothers did and rarely had to work things out for himself.

He loved being outdoors and showed particular talent at sports. His dad would frequently take Sam and his brothers to the park to play football – these occasions became something of a family tradition. At other times they would all go camping together, enjoying the challenges of building fires, walking and back packing.

From about the age of eight, Sam showed a real sensitivity for music. All the boys in the family had piano lessons, but Sam was able to improvise and make his own music very early on. He hated having to learn to read the music and in the end his mum and the piano teacher agreed that Sam should just be allowed to enjoy making music. Sam didn't see the need to read other people's music when he could make his own so easily.

Sam was looking forward to going to the big school – both of his brothers were there too, and both doing very well. He was excited by the possibilities of new friends and experiences. When he arrived there it was a bit of a shock to him that he was such a small fish in a very big pond. He felt a bit anonymous going from lesson to lesson and from teacher to teacher – a big change for someone who was used to an easy set of relationships in which he knew where he belonged. He began to look for ways to make himself feel noticed in his circle of friends.

Habib's story

Habib grew up as the fourth child in a family of seven. His dad ran his own business and his mother worked hard at home raising her children. There were uncles and grandparents living nearby and several cousins who all formed part of the same extended family. They worshipped regularly in the local mosque and the children in the family attended classes for young Muslims as well as participating in a range of social events provided by the community.

The family really valued education and saw it as an important means of getting on in life. Mother always supported the school, hearing children read and contributing in all sorts of ways to the Parent Teacher Association (PTA). There was a lot of conversation in the family and lots of debate at home and in the mosque about all sorts of issues, from politics through to religion and economics. Habib grew up in a context of active enquiry and engagement in life in the community. He modelled himself on his dad, who never took anything for granted.

When Habib began to show signs of struggling with reading and writing, the family responded by supporting him in finding his own strategies for overcoming his difficulties. Dad talked with him about how he could get round his difficulties and Habib never felt that *he* was the problem, just that he happened to find certain things more difficult than other children.

The school provided a lot of support for Habib too, and backed up the family's approach. It was quite clear that Habib was a very capable and well-motivated young man, who was interested in almost everything. He developed a very positive sense of himself as an active learner and experienced his world at home and at school as supportive and stimulating.

He had little patience with tasks that made no sense to him, or repeating things he already knew and would occasionally show considerable frustration when he was unable to follow his own interests. Sometimes he found school a little boring.

UNDERSTANDING OUR OWN LEARNING POWER

In order for Emma, Sam and Habib to become dynamic and effective learners they need three things:

- To become more aware of themselves as learners.
- To recognise and own their learning characteristics.
- To take responsibility for their own learning journey.

This may take a little while and it is likely that Habib will take to it more easily and quickly than Emma and Sam. They will need the support of their teachers and their parents and they will need to be in a learning community where the language of learning power is natural and normal.

In the next chapter we will look at these youngsters' learning profiles and will begin to understand how focusing on their learning power was an important means to help them become aware of their potential as learners and to take responsibility for their own learning.

Summary

In this chapter we have met Emma, Sam and Habib, three learners whose stories we will follow throughout this book.

We have seen how they each have different qualities and characteristics as learners and that they each have a particular story which has shaped the way they are and how they learn today.

In order to fulfil their potential, they need to become more aware of themselves as learners, to own their own learning identities and to take responsibility for their ongoing learning journey.

Typical learning profiles

In this chapter we delve more deeply into the three types of learners identified by the research – the types represented by Emma, Sam and Habib. We tell their stories and show how their learning profiles might help them and us to identify ways in which they can be supported in their capacity to learn and go on learning. First we discuss how a learning profile is assessed and then we meet our three learners.

- Dynamic personal assessment for learning.
- Fragile learners – recognising Emma.
- Vulnerable learners – recognising Sam.
- Effective learners – recognising Habib.

ASSESSING WHAT WE VALUE

We have now begun to understand something about the concept of learning power itself and its seven dimensions which are ways of identifying the quality of a person's engagement in his own learning processes. We have seen that learning power provides an important link between personal development and attainment for our students. Focusing our attention on learning power means that we can relate to the learner as a person as well as to what is being learned.

Teachers are assessing students formally and informally a great deal of the time. Good teaching requires good assessment. Finding ways to assess students' learning power, and to help students to assess themselves, is critically important for developing learning power in the classroom and beyond. It means assessing what we value, rather than only valuing what we can easily assess. Our assessment strategies should serve the purpose of learning and growth, rather than only labelling and grading.

ASSESSING LEARNING POWER

Finding ways to assess learning power is therefore important. The research base has provided a means to do this through a questionnaire that learners respond to. That questionnaire forms the basis of the ELLI Learning Profiles.

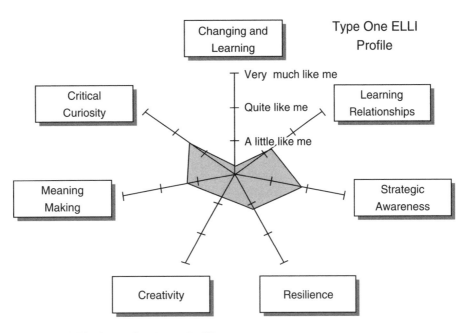

Figure 3.1   Individual Learning Power Profile

Students answer a range of questions about themselves, all of which provide information about how they perceive themselves in relation to each of the seven dimensions of learning power. They are asked 'How much like me is this?' It is all about how students think and feel about themselves as learners.

The learning profile questionnaire, which is usually completed 'online', then calculates how much of a particular learning power dimension a student reports him or herself to have at any one time. This is then converted into a percentage and produced in the form of a spider diagram with each of the spider's legs representing one of the seven dimensions of learning power. Look at Figure 3.1. You will notice that there are no numbers attached to this spider diagram. This is because numbers don't really help much as a form of feedback in this type of assessment – in fact they may actually make students think that they are not good enough rather than encouraging them to see how they can change. The learning profile is not about grading and comparing students, which is what numbers are most useful for. It is about providing feedback to learners which stimulates a response – **and it is the student's response to that feedback that is critical**.

> **Do we assess what we value or do we value what we assess?**
>
> If we believe that learning power is important for our young people, then we must find ways to assess it. This goes beyond formative assessment to students' assessment of themselves as learners.

The learning profiles invite three types of response from students:

- Awareness
- Ownership
- Responsibility.

RESPONSE-ABLE ASSESSMENT

One of the characteristics of learning power is that it cannot be assessed by what teachers think about a student. Unlike a performance or a test which can be judged by externally agreed criteria, teachers' judgements about learning power can only really be validated by what learners think and feel about themselves. It is a powerful form of self-assessment. This is sometimes difficult in a schooling system wedded to numbers and notions of objectivity.

- It is the student's **self-perception** that counts in providing the assessment information.
- It is the student's **self-awareness** that is important in the feedback.
- It is the student's **ownership of her own learning process** that matters in reflecting on the feedback from her learning profile.
- It is the student's capacity to take responsibility for her own learning journey that will make a difference to her capacity for learning.

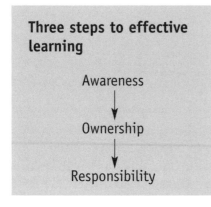

Three steps to effective learning

Awareness
↓
Ownership
↓
Responsibility

Self-awareness is the starting point, ownership comes next and taking responsibility is the desired outcome.

So we can see that the ELLI Learning Profiles are personal assessments, based on subjective information from learners. They are not private because they are influenced by the community and the relationships a learner finds him or herself a part of. They are not public either because they belong to the learner. Their purpose is dynamic personal development rather than public accountability.

The Learning Profiles provide a measure of 'how much' of a particular dimension a learner reports him or herself to have at any one time. The feedback produced for learners is in the form of a spider diagram. It is free of numbers and presents a profile of how the learner is on all of the dimensions together, rather than just looking at one thing. It is designed to be a stimulus for reflection and action rather than as a 'label' or a 'grade'.

In the next section we will look at the learning profiles completed by Emma, Sam and Habib. We will discuss the information that the learning profiles provide for us, and will present that information in the form of a story about our three learners. Most teachers already know a lot about their students – their backgrounds, their temperaments and characteristics in school and, of course, a lot about their attainment and other achievements. Interpreting individual learning profiles should always be done carefully and teachers will draw on their wider knowledge and professional discernment about the individual concerned. Ideally, the interpretation of a learning profile should include the individual concerned – and the profile should make sense for both the learner and the teacher. This 'making sense' of a learning profile is known as 'face validity'. The learning profile is merely a tool to give voice to what is already there – and the learner's and the teacher's judgements are as important as the profile itself.

Sometimes a learning profile will provide information that is surprising or unexpected. Research suggests that some students who are perceived as 'challenging' in school are actually very effective learners – it's just that that learning power is not channelled well in school. Others students may be very easy to have in class and may be high attainers but actually quite fragile and dependent as learners.

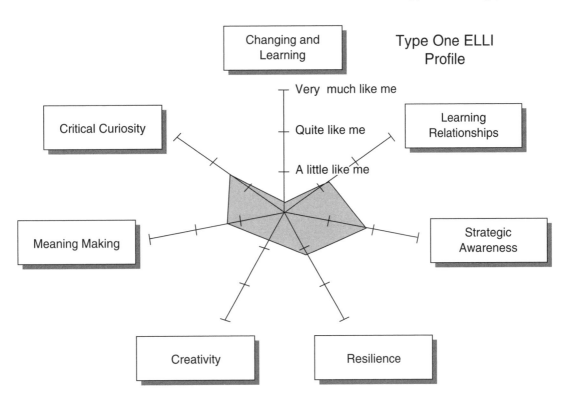

Figure 3.2   Emma's Learning Power Profile: typical of a fragile learner

We have already met Emma, Sam and Habib. They represent the most commonly identified types of learners. Getting to know them better as learners will help us to root these ideas about learning power in real life and to apply them in real classroom contexts.

INTRODUCING THREE TYPES OF LEARNERS

Research suggests that there are three main types of learners. These are:

- Fragile learners – weak on all learning power dimensions.
- Vulnerable learners – weak on some dimensions and strong on others.
- Strong learners – well rounded on all dimensions.

The following illustrations are based on real people, but the names Emma, Sam and Habib and some of the details are fictitious.

FRAGILE LEARNERS

The first type of learner we will discuss is the most fragile and dependent. Learners with this type of profile report themselves as not having very much of any of the seven dimensions of learning power. You can see from the shape of this learning profile that this learner's strongest area is Strategic Awareness, and her weakest area is Changing and Learning. Apart from Strategic Awareness, which reaches just over half-way to the maximum score, all of her scores are in the lower half of the scale.

Emma is an example of this type of learner. Her profile is shown in Figure 3.2.

Emma

The most significant element of Emma's identity as a learner is that she doesn't really believe that she can get better at learning. Deep down, she knows that however hard she tries she is unlikely to succeed and that she will never be as good as everyone else. She thinks she is not very clever and that is simply the way it is. And it will always be like that.

How Emma's characteristics as a learner relate to her story

- Whenever Emma finds something difficult, or she is confused, she takes this as evidence of her low ability and she is unlikely to try anything new because she does not want to risk failing again, and being seen to fail by her friends. She has two very successful older siblings, whom she compares herself to, and her family set a lot of store on high achievement. She feels the odd one out. She doesn't come over as fragile since she has many other strategies to compensate – she comes over as bored and somewhat disaffected. She has a reasonably strong sense of self, which is expressed in important ways outside of the classroom.
- Emma has a group of friends with whom she does feel safe and she tends to stick with these as far as she can, both in her learning and in her social life. She wants to be as like them as possible and looks to them a lot for help at school and at home. She is a good-looking young person and is particularly vulnerable to the attentions of older boys who can make her feel special very easily.
- Emma has become passive in her approach to school work, much preferring to be told what to do, and to reproduce the sort of work she believes is expected of her. As far as the curriculum is concerned, apart from her love of reading, she cannot see much point in it. She hasn't connected it with life outside school, or the news or current affairs, and the idea of a future career of some sort is very vague. She is not much trouble at school – just plodding along.
- One important feature of Emma's learning identity at the moment, however, and one which enables her to function in school without really being noticed too much, is her facility with language. She has always loved reading. Her mother used to read to her at home and she loves films and stories. She can often escape into another world through stories – and significantly this has led to an awareness of her own thoughts and feelings. She does reflect a little on what is going on around her, though not very much in school any more. It is this facility that she has used to reflect on her deficits, and to judge herself against external standards, finding herself wanting, rather than to reflect on her own sense of self and her capacity to learn.
- Actually, no one ever told Emma that she could get better at learning. Or that to be confused and to not know what to do is really quite normal – in fact if you know everything, you don't need to learn anything, so *not* knowing is very important. She has looked at her older brother and sister and her wider family and they have always seemed to be so confident and knowledgeable – and she has never seen them fail. Very different from her – or so she thinks.

- In her primary school as well as now, SATs results have always been terribly important. Since the school has been close to the top of the league tables it has been important for it to stay there – and being actually quite clever in some ways, she realised that the attention her teachers gave to certain students was to push them up into the next band for the sake of their test results rather than for their own sakes. She gets quite reasonable results herself, when she tries. Her actual performance, and the way others see her, is well 'out of sync' with her own perception of herself.

HOW COULD WE HELP EMMA?

- Emma would benefit from the support of a trusted teacher who can challenge her to change her perception of herself, through believing in her and creating a context in which she can succeed with real and achievable learning challenges and watch herself succeed. Her level of self-awareness and her love of language could be extended through self-assessment and taking responsibility for her own choices in learning. She is well able to understand the language of learning power and, through metaphor and in other ways, to use these concepts for herself.
- By beginning to understand that learning is learnable and with careful choice of subject matter that is meaningful to her, she may well be able to develop strategies and processes to help herself succeed. Friends matter to her, and creating situations for collaborative learning and challenge, rather than dependency, may be a key for Emma. Her parents may well be able to help, since they may realise that she rather puts herself down, or they may need some support themselves in understanding how to help. In any event, engaging Emma in dialogue about her identity as a learner is an important starting point.

VULNERABLE LEARNERS

The second type of learning profile we will call 'vulnerable' because learners of this type are strong in some dimensions, but weaker in others, and therefore vulnerable, especially to changes in their learning environment. They are typical of the sorts of learners who may not be noticed much in school, but who are at risk of switching off from formal learning and not developing their own aspirations and challenges.

Sam

As you can see from Sam's learning profile (Figure 3.3), his strongest dimension is Changing and Learning where he reaches the maximum possible. He is, however, comparatively weak on Strategic Awareness, Resilience and Critical Curiosity.

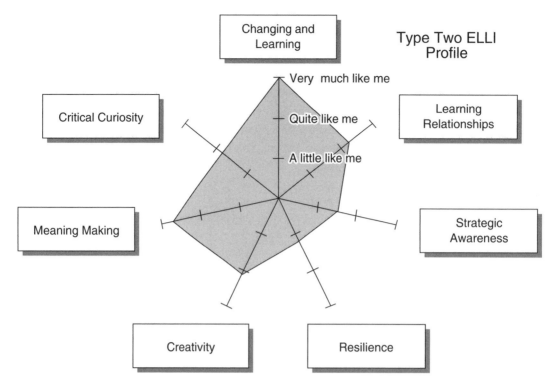

Figure 3.3 Sam's Learning Power Profile: typical of a vulnerable learner

Sam is a smashing kid. The sort you would be pleased to have in any class. He is eleven years old and is in Year 7 having just come up to the big school from a very happy and productive primary school experience. He is the youngest boy in a family where there is lots of support.

How Sam's characteristics as a learner relate to his story

- Sam has a very positive sense of himself as a learner and his experience to date has shown him that he can grow and develop with effort over time. He is bright and good at the sort of learning needed for school tests. He sees learning as something he will be doing for many years to come and probably for the rest of his life. His parents have been doing further studies and formal learning is 'normal' in his household.

- Sam loves to find out about things that matter to him – and football is up there at the top of the list. He likes to make sense of new information, and makes an effort to apply his learning to new situations. He is well disposed towards learning in school at the moment, and tries to make sense of what he encounters in his different lessons.

- However, in a number of lessons there are tell-tale signs that much of what Sam does in school does not really connect with his own life and experience. He doesn't put a lot of effort into his homework – the main goal is to get it done. He finds it difficult to stay on task in class and can often be seen daydreaming or chatting to his friends.

- Sam is a popular boy who gets on well with his friends and loves being with them. He knows that he can work on his own when necessary and is excellent in group situations. He is pretty balanced in his learning relationships – he has people at home and in his community who will help him when he needs them, and he knows that he can work things out for himself if he has to.

- The most vulnerable area for Sam is his lack of resilience and his limited strategic awareness of himself as a learner. When he encounters problems he tends to give up easily. Being the youngest son in the family he is used to having things done for him – and he will easily give up when the going gets tough. He has not realised that being confused and having to try really hard is an essential part of learning – and indeed of life – and that he can manage those feelings for himself. He actually finds those sorts of feelings difficult and just wants them to go away, rather than to tolerate them and work with them.

- He doesn't plan much at all – he will often launch into a task without thinking and he will often forget to bring things he needs into school. His lack of 'strategic awareness' also means that when he finds lessons boring or meaningless, he doesn't know how to make them interesting or fun – by asking questions, or getting his learning needs met – so he resorts to messing around! For example, in French he has to learn a set of words which have no relevance to him at all – they don't even fit together. He sees his teachers as providing him with information and things to do rather than seeing himself as responsible for his own learning.

- Sam is at quite a vulnerable stage in Year 7. He is growing up fast – though not as fast as the girls in his class – and is increasingly influenced by friends around him. He is finding the challenge of making sense of the curriculum increasingly difficult and is beginning to 'switch off' in significant ways. As his attainment drops and he begins to get into trouble with his teachers for not doing his homework or not remembering things, his confidence in himself as a learner will be undermined. He is unlikely to get noticed because he is right in the middle of the class – even his 'misbehaviour' is pretty mild compared to others.

How could we help Sam?

- Sam really needs his teachers to help make his curriculum meaningful to him, and to introduce him to the language of learning so that he can begin to understand that he can take responsibility for himself. In particular he will benefit from becoming aware that he, Sam, can develop his learning muscles by training them, just as he develops his body in football training. He can learn to ask questions, to use his imagination and find more sophisticated ways of making sense of his learning. He needs the support to become resilient enough to ask questions, to think things through, to make connections and to allow his creativity to inform his learning. Giving Sam choice about what he is learning will be very important – as will be supporting him in planning and developing larger-scale projects which will begin to build up the strategic awareness and self-knowledge he needs to learn well.

EFFECTIVE LEARNERS

The third type of learner is the effective learner. Learners like this report themselves to have lots of each of the seven dimensions when they respond to their learning profiles – and they are pretty equally balanced. These learners may not

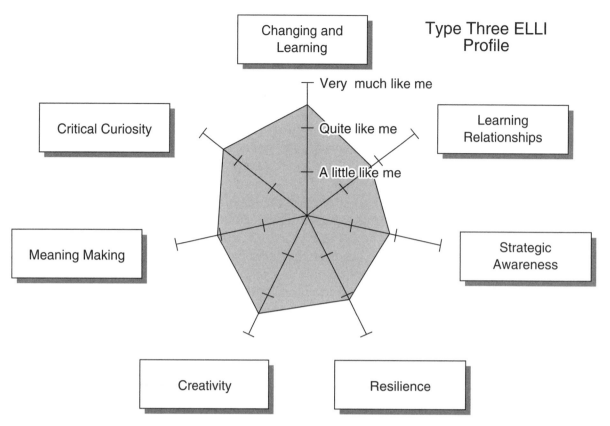

Figure 3.4 Habib's Learning Power Profile: typical of an effective learner

be high attainers, but they are fulfilling their potential and getting the most out of their learning.

● Habib

Habib is the youngest of our learners. He is nine and he is in Year 5. Although he has a mild form of dyslexia, the story of his life has been a positive one where there have always been people around him who have supported him in his learning and growing. He has several brothers and sisters and a large extended family. He attends the local mosque, where there are often classes for Habib and his friends and a wide range of community activities.

● How Habib's characteristics as a learner relate to his story

● Habib's learning profile (shown in Figure 3.4) suggests that he is pretty well rounded on all of the learning dimensions. He is actively engaged in his learning and loves going to school. Despite finding spellings and writing difficult he has learned to find strategies to overcome this and it does not impede his creativity or engagement with learning. His parents found him specialist tuition for this disability and his teachers have always taken it seriously and supported Habib in adapting at school.

● It may be that his learning disability has helped Habib to become the effective learner that he is. He learned that even though he finds some tasks difficult, there is always a way round them. Learning to persevere has been very important for him, as has learning to draw his self-esteem from his ability to overcome, rather than from a perfect performance. He has several important relationships where teachers, siblings and community members have supported him and encouraged his resilience. In his school, there is a 'no put down' policy which has been very effective so that it has provided him with a safe environment in which to be himself.

- Habib is naturally curious, and constantly seeking to understand what is going on around him. He finds that he can use his imagination and often, if he just relaxes and waits, solutions will emerge in his mind. Sometimes his active curiosity means that he has to learn to keep quiet in class rather than constantly ask questions and he has to learn to listen to others. He is actually very capable and this can mean that he is sometimes impatient with his friends who are not so motivated or engaged. He has had to learn to listen to other people carefully and to value their contributions. He is an expert helper for other children – and gains self-esteem and develops his own learning by supporting others.

How could we help Habib?

- While Habib reports himself as pretty effective as a learner, at least at the time he did his learning profile, there is no room for complacency. He needs to continue to experience enough success in learning to maintain this positive learning identity. Even though he succeeds well in regular classroom assessments and performs well towards the top end of grades, this should not be taken for granted. In particular he could be encouraged to deepen his awareness of himself as a learner and to plan and develop projects which extend him, both in the content and in the process of learning.

LEARNING IDENTITIES

We have now met three individual learners and have presented their stories. We could go into much greater depth in this way – as a teacher you are likely to have much more information about your students that will help you to build up a clearer picture of their learning identities.

There are at least four themes that contribute to these profiles:

Learning capacities: the skills, dispositions and awarenesses a learner will tend to make use of as she learns.

> *Emma, for example, is disposed to simply do what she is told to do – and she is pretty skilled at that, whereas Sam will 'play around' with mind maps in order to understand. Habib tends to always ask pertinent questions.*

Learning identity: what a person thinks and feels about him or herself as a learner.

Habib is pretty confident that he can get where he wants to go and feels good about himself; Sam is beginning to feel that he may not be a very good learner in school because he is finding it boring; and Emma deeply believes that she is not good at learning at all.

Learning relationships: the quality of relationships that a person has with important others.

Emma tends to be dependent on her teachers and her friends; Sam is able to learn with others as well as on his own, though he tends to allow himself to be shaped by other people's opinions; and Habib is able to stand on his own two feet in learning but at the same time gets a lot of learning support from others. He is particularly good at coaching his friends because he instinctively knows what will help.

Learning story: the memories and experiences that individuals bring to their learning, and their hopes and aspirations for the future.

Emma's role in her family has very much shaped who she is today – growing up comparing herself to her siblings has not been good for her. Sam's story is a positive one – plenty of support and good modelling at home; and Habib's extended family and community traditions have helped to shape his story in a very positive way.

In the next chapter we will explore class profiles. These are individual learning profiles which are amalgamated for a whole class. We will look at the ways teachers can respond to those profiles by adjusting how they teach, rather than what they teach, in order to address the learning needs identified in the class profiles.

Summary

In this chapter we introduced individual learning profiles and recognised our three young learners as typical of the types of learners identified in our research.

- We discussed how the assessment of learning power is based on students' self-perception and that it is the students' response to the feedback that matters.
- Self-assessment is an important way to develop the awareness, ownership and responsibility students need to become effective learners.
- We saw how Emma, Sam and Habib represent three different types of learners and related their learning profiles to their stories.
- We saw how a person's learning profile is made up of learning capacities, learning identity, learning relationships and learning stories

 FURTHER READING

Flutter, J. and Ruddick, J. (2004) *Consulting Pupils: What's in It for Schools?* London: Routledge Falmer.

Chapter 4

Creating a learner-centred classroom

We have looked at the individual learning profiles of Emma, Sam and Habib. Now we will look at what we can learn if we combine individual learning power profiles and look at the learning characteristics of a whole class of students. We will discover that:

- learning generally takes place in a complex web of relationships
- groups of students have particular learning characteristics
- teachers can adjust their learning and teaching strategies to suit a particular class.

The climate of a classroom has a profound impact on the quality of learning that takes place within it. We have already seen that a classroom that is 'learner centred' provides a hospitable climate in which learning power can develop, whereas a classroom that is overly controlled, or centred mostly on passing tests, is likely to depress students' learning power.

We also know that the quality of relationships between students in the classroom will have an impact on their learning. Take Sam, for instance. He is gradually switching off from key parts of the curriculum and increasingly being influenced by what his friends think and feel about him, and about school. His relative lack of *resilience* means that he is likely to take the easy way out, becoming dependent on others and allowing himself to be shaped more by the group than by his own learning needs and aspirations.

CLASS LEARNING PROFILES

When a whole class completes a learning profile online, then we can see the average score for the whole class on each learning dimension. The profile is presented as a histogram or bar chart, which also shows the number of students in each 'bracket' or 'score range'. The profiles use the traffic light system – those students represented by the red bars are students whose profiles put them in the lowest rating for that dimension. These are the students who need immediate attention in that domain. Students whose scores are in the middle rating for a particular dimension are represented by yellow bars. These students need to be encouraged and monitored in that particular dimension. Students whose scores are in the highest rating for a particular dimension are represented by green bars. They could be used to coach and advise their peers in the strategies and actions that contribute to their strength in this area.

Interpreting a class learning profile

Take a careful look at the class learning profile in Figure 4.1. Reflect on what sort of information this gives you about this class's learning power. Which areas cause most concern? Who are the students who stand out from the rest? Does this profile fit with what you know about the class?

This sort of information can be very useful for teachers in understanding the 'learning personality' of the class as a whole. There are particular patterns that emerge which in turn suggest particular responses and strategies from teachers.

The class learning profile presented in Figure 4.1 is typical. Let's imagine that this is Sam's class, a Year 7 science group. As you can see from the class profile there are thirteen students who report themselves as having a strong sense of *changing and learning*, and we know that Sam must be one of them. There are five members of the class, however, whose scores are in the lowest rating in this dimension, with very poor images of themselves as able to learn and grow over time. One in particular is significantly at risk in this area. While this is important information, the dimension of learning power which is most troubling is Strategic Awareness, where there are no students who report themselves as being strongly strategically aware. Not far behind this are the areas of Creativity and then Critical Curiosity.

If we take the whole-class profile together we can begin to make some suggestions about the learning 'personality' of the whole class. As a group they are fairly confident in themselves as learners. They have positive relationships with each other and they like their teacher, for whom they will generally work hard. It is probably considered to be a pleasant class to teach because they will engage with tasks they are given and generally work well together. However, taken as a whole, they may be somewhat passive in their approach to learning, being keener to follow instructions and to be told how to go about things rather than finding out for themselves or experimenting. Perhaps they have come to believe that learning in school is about getting the right answers and passing the test, rather than using their initiative find things out for themselves. There is typically a queue to the teacher's desk of students wanting help. Rarely do the students come up with their own answers, pose questions or offer alternative ways of looking at problems.

In particular they lack a language for the processes of learning itself, tending to focus on the grades they get for their work, or their teachers' comments, rather than on how they can improve what they have done. Generally they don't have much fun learning – fun is what happens in the playground or at the weekend.

Lets have a closer look at the bar charts.

Changing and Learning

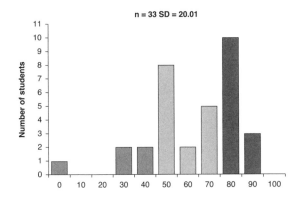

n = 33 SD = 20.01

The red bars are those students who rate themselves as 'pretty stuck' and not likely to change. There are 5 of them altogether. There are 13 students who think they are changing and learning a lot and 15 who are in the middle. So about half the class could do with support in seeing themselves as 'changers and learners'…

Critical Curiosity

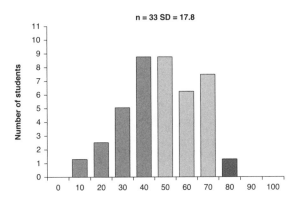

n = 33 SD = 17.8

… while only one of the students thinks he has lots of critical curiosity and 14 are definitely in the 'red'. As a group, they seem rather unquestioning.

Meaning Making

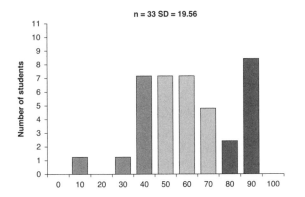

n = 33 SD = 19.56

Nine students are strong on meaning making, but the majority are not making as much sense out of school as we might hope.

Creativity

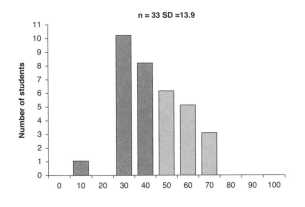

n = 33 SD =13.9

In the same class, there are no students who perceive themselves to use their creativity in learning very much – not much use of imagination, intuition and risk taking – and the majority of students (19) report themselves to be 'in the red' on this dimension.

Figure 4.1 *(Continued)*

Strategic Awareness

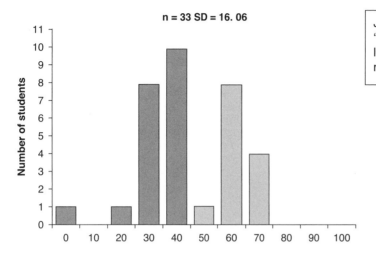

n = 33 SD = 16. 06

> Just as worrying, the majority are just 'going along' without reflecting on their learning processes and developing awareness of themselves as learners ...

Resilience

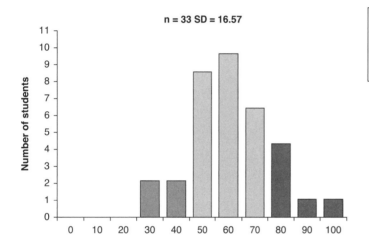

n = 33 SD = 16.57

> ... however, they are still pretty resilient on the whole and also there seems to be a number of students with the capacity for positive learning relationships.

Learning Relationships

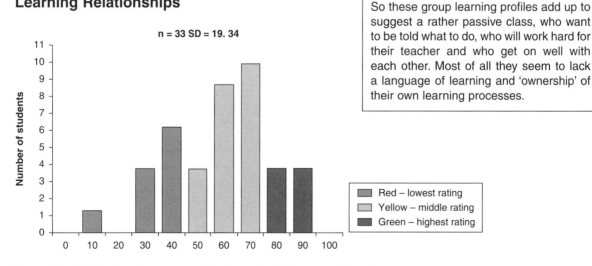

n = 33 SD = 19. 34

> So these group learning profiles add up to suggest a rather passive class, who want to be told what to do, who will work hard for their teacher and who get on well with each other. Most of all they seem to lack a language of learning and 'ownership' of their own learning processes.

Red – lowest rating
Yellow – middle rating
Green – highest rating

Figure 4.1 Whole-class learning profiles for each of the seven dimensions

RESPONDING TO CLASS LEARNING PROFILES

Sam's teacher, Dominic, uses the assessment data presented in these learning profiles to inform his learning and teaching strategies for this particular class. This does not necessarily mean doing something completely different to what is already planned within a scheme of work – it means doing the same thing differently.

Doing the same thing differently

Building learning power in the classroom is about responding to the specific learning needs of students, rather than providing a different curriculum.

Death by worksheet

Mary's Year 6 class were working hard towards their SATs assessments. They loved Mary and worked hard for her and for their parents. They were optimistic and set to do well. However, their learning profiles showed them to be very passive indeed and significantly lacking in strategic awareness.

As soon as Mary saw their learning profiles, she began to unsettle the class by challenging them to solve problems for themselves or with each other. She abandoned worksheets and began to reward 'softer' virtues relating to learning power. She introduced the language of learning power and of self-assessment and began to require her students to track their own progress. It was a little more uncomfortable for everyone, but it paid off in terms of the students' engagement and enjoyment of learning, and they achieved excellent results in their SATs for good measure!

For example, on the scheme of work for this term there is a topic on the earth's climate in relation to the sun. Rather than simply being given the information about the earth's relationship to the sun, Dominic sets the topic up as a problem to be solved which would require the students to use higher order creative and critical thinking skills.

However, the students in this class also appear to lack a language of learning and the capacity to reflect on their learning processes. So, as well as setting a learning objective at the beginning of the lesson which has to do with understanding the relationship between the earth and the sun, Dominic sets a learning objective which relates to the process of learning. So, for example:

In this lesson we will:

- understand how the position of the sun relates to the earth's climate
- develop our critical curiosity and our creativity.

As well as sequencing the information content of the curriculum differently, Dominic is being explicit about the importance and value of curiosity and creativity. He is inviting the students to reflect upon their own capacity for changing and growing in these dimensions of learning power by applying them to the task in hand.

By setting aside time for personal evaluation and target setting during the lesson he is creating a context which encourages self-awareness, ownership and responsibility for learning.

Finally, Dominic knows from individual learning profiles and from his own experience which students are weakest in learning relationships, and he is able to set the students to learn in groups which facilitate positive learning relationships and encourage students to learn how to problem solve with each other.

It is important to consider all the dimensions of learning power as part of a whole, bearing in mind that a focus on one dimension, such as Strategic Awareness or Resilience, will lead to the explicit encouragement of other dimensions. To change and learn a student needs to know where she is going and how to get there, which requires strategic awareness and critical curiosity and so on. To become critically curious a student needs to be able to make meaning, and to become aware of himself as a learner. The dimensions are always part of a whole, and should not be focused on in complete isolation from each other.

Each class's learning power profile is unique, in the same way that each individual's learning power profile is unique. However, it is possible to identify trends and types of class profiles and to look at learning profile data on a larger scale for, say, a whole year group, or a school.

It is not unusual to find class profiles where there is a relative lack of strategic awareness which is accompanied by a passive learning profile – that is, one which is weaker on critical curiosity and creativity. The children in these classes may well be high attainers and easy to teach. Ben's 'A' level biology class described in Chapter 1 is one such example. The next four chapters have more practical ideas and stories about the sorts of things teachers do in the classroom to support students in developing their own learning power.

KEY FACTORS IN THE ECOLOGY OF LEARNING IN THE CLASSROOM

The ecology of learning power, which we described in Chapter 1, is a complex and sensitive web of values and practices which are expressed in the context of relationships in the classroom. These create a tangible climate which nurtures or inhibits learning. Research suggests that there are a number of key themes which are important, and which we can attend to as we aim to create a learner-centred climate which fosters the development of each of the dimensions of learning power.

Teacher commitment to learner-centred values, and willingness to make professional judgements

> Self-evaluating teachers create learner-centred classrooms

Building learning power in the classroom is dependent on the vision and values of the teacher and his or her capacity for *changing and learning* as a professional. Without a commitment on the part of the teacher to be open to new learning and new data there is little chance of the sort of dynamism and energy in the classroom that will foster resilient learners.

When a teacher receives a learning profile for an individual or for a class as a whole it is not a static piece of data. It is part of a process of student self-assessment and it requires interpretation. This requires the teacher to use her professional judgement, drawing on her experience of these particular students and evidence from a range of sources.

There is neither a single formula nor a single list of strategies that can be applied across the board. The key is in the teacher's professional inspiration for learning and her commitment to being learner centred.

Thus a creative pedagogy which responds uniquely to each learning challenge is what is required. This cannot be forced into a 'learnacy hour' or any particular straitjacket – though such structures may be found helpful and appropriate for particular needs.

Positive relationships characterised by trust, affirmation and challenge

Relationships are the currency of learning power, such that we could describe this approach as 'relational learning'. Learning power is nurtured within a complex web of relationships. In the classroom the most obvious relationships are those between the teacher and students and among the students themselves.

However, equally significant is a student's relationship with himself. The relationship I have with myself endures over time and has been profoundly shaped by other key relationships – with my parents, my family and my community. The traditions or stories that shape my culture and my community also play a part in my sense of identity.

Right at the heart of the idea of learning power is a student's sense of herself as a learner. It's about self-perception and awareness, taking ownership of her own learning process and taking responsibility for her own learning. If our teaching and learning strategies don't encourage this sort of personalisation of learning, then they are not really learner centred.

Human brains are 'hardwired' to find meaning, identity and purpose in the context of relationships. When students enter the classroom they carry these webs of relationships with them. The quality of relationships that the teacher and school are able to create is critically important. We know when we experience a good relationship although it is hard to measure. Positive relationships are a product of who people *are*, as well as what they *do*. Attending to the inner life of the teacher as well as to his capacity for building healthy relationships is part of what it means to be learner centred.

Time and story matter. My story is one of the most significant ways in which I make meaning out of my life. My story has a past, a present and a future, which shape my hopes and aspirations. And my story is enacted in the context of relationships.

Research shows that trust, affirmation and challenge are key ingredients of effective learning relationships. Trust is a hallmark of a relationship of such quality that both parties are confident that it can withstand the challenges of inequality, risk, uncertainty and difference.[1]

'Golden moments' in learning relationships

Jane's class of ten-year-olds proved to be weak in learning relationships. Jane put them into balanced ability groups, working with others they did not usually work with, and used story as a teaching strategy. She noticed that people who have an effect on the students or who are special to them also tell those students stories about themselves. She told her students that *'we are the stories we tell ourselves'* and that *'telling my story in the classroom'* helps me to make sense of who I am and where I belong. Students began to tell their stories to each other. Jane describes the following 'golden moment':

> *One of the most significant moments was a mini-topic week we had in January. The children worked in teams which I had selected. They didn't have their special friends in their teams. They worked for the whole week with children they had hardly spoken to before. It astounded me that they could have been in a class since they were five years old and never really communicated with some of the other children. However, in this week, those barriers were broken down and the children recognised that this had happened. They discovered that they could enjoy school and learn with anyone, not just their friends. They recognised the value of working with a team, negotiating, reflecting on one another's strengths and using them. They realised that sharing learning is fun and productive.*

How teachers use their power in the classroom, how they create a safe environment where students are not afraid of being put down, how they manage risk and uncertainty are all part of building trust and affirmation. When they are in place, then *changing and learning* are much easier and challenge can be supported.

Learning, by definition, involves uncertainty and risk and change. In order to learn something, you have to 'not know it' beforehand. Not knowing can be uncertain and risky – and what is often at risk is one's self-esteem. Creating safe relationships which facilitate risk taking and change is all part of being learner centred.

In order to learn something, the learner has to move beyond his 'comfort zone' and often has to face uncertainty and risk. Furthermore the teacher often *does* know, where the learner *does not*, and this represents an unequal balance of power. The characteristic of trust, or the confidence that these things can be faced, and negotiated, and that the relationship will not break down through abuse, or fragility, appears to be a critical thread in the ecology of a learner-centred environment.

Dominic's science department in an inner city comprehensive school identified the following teaching principles which underpin a learner-centred approach:

'Golden Moments' for learning buddies

When buddy pairs had to look at plants and flowers to plan a window box, one effective learner went to find an adult gardening book in the classroom so that his non-reading companion could look at the plants for planning.

Although he preferred to work independently he was aware of the needs of the other and was prepared to work at a slower pace, showing understanding and empathy. Both were proud of their outcomes and design.

- Creating a secure environment through structure and nurture, through valuing students' views and opinions, operating a 'no put down' policy, and attending to interpersonal problems.
- Commitment to supportive question and answer sessions – that is, questions that both challenge and affirm individuals, with attempts being made to value all contributions.

Mary developed a 'Buddy System' in her class of seven-year-olds and used this to focus on developing *changing and learning* and *resilience*.

She used ELLI Learning Profile data to pair students who were generally dependent learners with those who were generally interdependent learners and put them together as 'learning buddies' engaged on particular learning tasks. The explicit focus was on developing a learning dialogue between the paired individuals, which was 'co-operative' and where both were able to contribute. Examples of work representing a positive process of collaborative learning were put on display.

Learning activities were structured to require communication and collaboration in planning, finding out, analysing and presenting ideas. One activity described by the teacher was a task involving reading and discussing the instructions on the back of seed packets. The activities for the pair were to:

- Investigate, using evidence from three seed packets, what sort of information manufacturers give about sowing seeds.
- To make statements or questions sharing this learning.
- To take it in turns to record findings.
- To give subheadings using facts found.
- To share ideas with the whole class.

The task led to significant discussion and negotiation between the students about how to do the task, how to present it, what were the main ideas and so on.

Developing a language of learning

Asking children what they think about learning is often very revealing. One ten-year-old described learning as '*a kind of course you do for twelve years*' and thought learning was about '*preparing you for a job*'. More positively, others said '*we never stop learning*' and '*My mum is 39 and she learns off me*' and '*you need to trust yourself to be a learner*'.

Without words to describe different aspects of learning power it is hard for learners to name their experiences and to become self-aware and responsible learners. The introduction of the language of learning into the classroom provides an important foundation for a learner-centred climate and it is always more effective when it is owned and appropriated by the learners themselves.

Teachers have used strategies such as 'mind mapping' with students to identify what they think are the qualities of effective learners. They then introduce the seven dimensions of learning power and students choose their own names for the dimensions. The language can be distinctive in each classroom – it is the ideas, and the ownership of the ideas, that really matter.

Here is an example from a class of nine-year-olds. They chose a new word for each learning power dimension – two words for learning relationships.

- **Grower**: someone who knows she can get better at learning.
- **Connector**: someone who is able to use what she already knows to help her solve problems and understand things that are new to her. Someone who links learning to life.

- **Curious**: someone who wants to ask questions and who enjoys discovering new things. Someone who wonders 'who', 'why', 'what', 'where', 'how', 'when', etc.
- **Playful**: someone who is able to look at things in different ways and who likes to solve problems and explore new ideas. Someone who doesn't mind making mistakes and enjoys learning.
- **Reflective**: someone who likes the time to think and who thinks before and after she acts. Someone who questions what she does and thinks of the way that she has been learning and what she needs to do to become a better learner.
- **Team worker**: someone who can work with others. Someone who can listen, is not bossy, can co-operate. Someone who does her share of the work, will make suggestions but is able to appreciate what others say and do.
- **Independent**: someone who can work on her own. Someone who does not need a teacher standing over her to begin, carry on with and complete a piece of work. Someone who is organised, can follow instructions and tackle a task without needing constant assistance or reassurance.
- **Tenacious**: someone who likes a challenge, can stick at problems, thinks of what to do when she gets stuck. Someone who understands that learning can be hard but will still have a go.

Using metaphors and similes

Every teacher we have worked with in the research has made use of learning metaphors with their classes. Metaphor is integral to understanding and learning and we use metaphors consistently in everyday life, both in our thinking and in our behaviour.[2] Metaphors and similes are about understanding and experiencing one kind of thing in terms of another and they profoundly shape our view of life and our aspirations for the future.

Learning power is an invisible quality of human beings, but it can be readily accessed through metaphor by very young children. Metaphors and similes open new possibilities in the minds of children and connect with them at a number of levels, whereas talking with students about learning in a conventional or theoretical way does not have the same effect.

You will read about some powerful metaphors using animals in Chapter 6 where each learning power dimension is named as an animal with particular characteristics. We can all identify with animals, and endow them with particular characteristics, and when those animals come to life as puppets in the classroom then they can powerfully support the ownership of a language of learning.

Percy Vere: the driver of the learning train

Teachers have no limits to their creativity when it comes to developing metaphors for learning power. Meet Percy Vere who is the driver of the learning train which travels over the tracks of relationships. Percy Vere has to bring his passengers along with him and they often have to stop off for a tea break, and to reflect on which track to go down next …

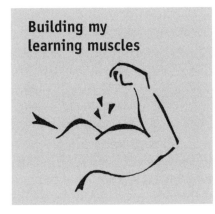

**Building my
learning muscles**

In another classroom students are 'building their learning muscles' and working out in the 'learning gym', practising pushing through the 'pain barriers' to 'reach their goals'.

Yet another class are writing their own 'learning is like ...' similes. 'Learning is like ... driving on a motorway. Sometimes you are in the fast lane and other times you are in the slow lane'; 'Learning is like ... your heart. It never stops beating'. Try making up your own 'learning is like ...' similes.

Modelling and imitation

The dimensions of learning power are present in the values, dispositions and attitudes of learners. That means they can be identified by what people think, feel and do in relation to their learning. Unlike memorising a set of rules, learning power is engendered in the experiences of participating in the daily life of a learning community. As a classroom becomes a learner-centred community, students interact with each other, with their teachers and with the tasks in hand. They tune into their learning on a number of levels and imitation is a key way in which people become immersed in particular learning practices. The fact that some families are mini-learning communities in their own right probably explains why some children already have high levels of learning power at a very young age. How people are, how they behave and what they do is as important as what they say. In fact young people often have a very finely tuned 'radar' facility which enables them to spot when teachers' actions don't match their words. They will imitate people they admire and trust.

Teachers in this context are the leading learners and modelling this in practice is critically important. Students need to know that teachers also feel unsure sometimes, don't know the answers and have to learn *resilience*. A learner-centred teacher is a co-learner, rather than the repository and judge of all knowledge.

Dominic, our science teacher, modelled higher order thinking by 'thinking out loud' and encouraging students to join in. He talked about the ways in which he managed his feelings as he demonstrated a 'learner friendly' way of coping with failure. Teachers can share their personal experiences and stories about learning, using role play and story, and they can be honest and open about their own limitations.

Rather than cheating, imitation is an important strategy for learning and students can learn from each other through imitation. Weaker students can watch stronger students do something, and then imitate it. Conversations between the teacher and a learner, about particular learning processes, can be 'listened in on' by the rest of the class as a way of exemplifying some learning processes.

Learning dialogues

Dialogue means speaking as a listener

Dialogue is more than just talking to each other. Dialogue requires that each party listens to the other and respects the other person's contribution. In other words there is a requirement to 'speak as a listener'. Dialogue flourishes in the context of relationships characterised by trust, affirmation and challenge and it is diminished when there is fear of being put down or not being heard. Sometimes academic conversation is really a power game of 'my idea is bigger than yours!' when the ruling metaphor is one of a 'battle'. Dialogue is best characterised by a 'dance' metaphor, when one person does one thing, then another person responds and the intricate set of moves adds up to a unique, creative act. Each contribution is essential to, and part of, the whole.

The quality of dialogue in the classroom is diagnostic of its level of learner centredness. All of the learning dimensions are nurtured through dialogue – whether that is stimulating curiosity, brainstorming creative solutions, making meaning or reflecting together on my learning progress.

Dialogue can take place in whole-class discussion, small groups and in ones and twos. Dialogue can be focused on the learning task in hand where there is a group commitment to problem solving and it can be a means of reflecting on the process of learning as well: a sort of meta-learning conversation.

Sam was working in a problem-solving group to develop a model of how the sun goes around the earth. He and his learning partners had to be creative, critical and resilient to develop the best hypothesis and build a model.

Afterwards the whole class held a dialogue about the different hypotheses AND about how the team had utilised the seven dimensions of learning power.

Their teacher was able to challenge fixed and negative perceptions and to value creativity and critical thinking. The students experienced the process of learning together and learned how to listen and respect 'the other'.

Time for reflection

Time for reflection is to learning power what eating is to living. Yet it is time that is so often lacking in most classrooms, as teachers struggle to meet external demands.

Time is important – but so is space. Having the time is a start, but if during that time learners are distracted by other things – events at home, personal issues, or stress about exams – then they will not be able to reflect meaningfully on learning.

Creating time and space for reflection is a special skill. Students need to feel safe and valued in order to contribute. There are classroom rituals and symbols that can be created which help and there are skills and techniques, such as those associated with meditation, which may be usefully deployed. Circle time, where students sit round with their teacher, with a view to listening and talking and reflecting about the day, is a particularly useful strategy.

Student self-assessment

In order to become self-evaluating learners, students must firstly become self-aware, then they must 'own' their own learning profiles and then take responsibility for their learning journey. These are the ingredients of self-assessment of learning power.

Learning jigsaws

Mary's Year 6 class each had a learning jigsaw on the wall. Each piece of the jigsaw represented a learning dimension. When students felt they had achieved what they set out to do in any dimension, then they could add that piece of the jigsaw.

One child who found concentration hard and rarely contributed put up his hand and asked two really good questions. His target at that time was to become more curious. He was one of the least able in the class and was genuinely delighted with himself and interested.

It means that learners are leading participants, facilitated by expert learners – their teachers. In all classrooms where we have developing learning power, student self-assessment is a key theme. In the secondary classrooms these strategies are often very similar to assessment for learning, although the purpose of self-assessment of learning power is for learning itself, rather than for subject performance. In the primary classrooms there is sometimes more space for highly creative and idiosyncratic responses.

One such response was a visual tool for self-assessment in which a wall display of a learning jigsaw was colour coded, with each part representing one of the learning dimensions. As a student made progress along a particular dimension – say he became consistently more curious – he would add the 'curious' piece into the jigsaw puzzle. The students' jigsaws were placed on the wall as a constant visual reminder of the goals of their learning journey. Learners identified their own targets for change and these were reviewed regularly with the teacher in a time set aside each fortnight for this purpose. The teachers took care to stress that it was not a race, but rather something that should be taken at the pace of each learner.

Here Dominic describes how self-assessment worked informally in science:

During the science activity students were asked to identify patterns which could form the basis for an investigation. A number of students were finding the activity very hard. I then asked them to think about resilience in their learning profile and pointed out that this activity would help build resilience and that it was as important to try as it was to achieve the outcome. Normally without this input the students would have come off task, but instead they re-focused and tried much harder. Though many of them did not succeed in the task at the end of the activity they were not dispirited as they felt they had succeeded in the area of resilience.

More formal approaches to self-assessment for learning power include students writing a learning journal which describes their learning power achievements; including a learning power goal in regular school target-setting process; finding and producing evidence for when they have met a target; writing this down or telling the class; engaging in a mentoring relationship where they are coached in a particular dimension ... the list goes on. For very young children, digital cameras can be used to take a photograph of a particular event – this photograph can then be included in the production of a 'learning story book', or put on display for 'star learners'.

Providing students with choice

Making choices is important for having an identity and a sense of ownership. We value what we choose as human beings, and the less choice we actually have in life, the more important small choices become. Students don't have any choice about going to school, or being in a particular class. Giving them choice within the class is an important sign of trust and respect and supports the development of identity and responsibility.

Sometimes choices can be very simple. Annie had a class of fourteen-year-olds whom she taught English. They were a top set, but were very passive and dependent, constantly asking her for solutions. She set up a situation where they had a number of choices they could make before asking her. She says this:

Levels of resilience in the group were low; most would almost always immediately ask me for help if they were stuck, without really trying to reach an answer themselves. This would be obvious, for example, in requesting help for spelling; very few would attempt to spell the word themselves before asking for help, and would then expect me to provide the correct answer for them. In most lessons I found I was the first 'port of call' when they got stuck; they would call for me or raise their hands before really thinking for themselves.

I set up a lesson with a set of progressively more difficult questions for group work; this was to ensure the first few were easy enough to build their confidence. Before the groups began work, I explained, and wrote on the board, the steps they should take if they got stuck. First was to use dictionaries and other reference books I placed around the room. Second was to ask each other. Third was to ask someone in another group. Fourth was to use clues I had written for each question, and placed on my desk. Lastly was to ask me, but I told them I would not help if they could not demonstrate that they had gone through the previous steps.

I was not asked to provide answers once during this lesson. When I analysed the groups' work, their answers were correct. I observed pupils following the strategies for support; only one group availed themselves of the clues. I cannot recall a previous lesson with this group when I have not been called on for help, or for reassurance.

● Creating challenge through re-sequencing the content

How the content of the curriculum is sequenced and framed is very important in developing learning power. Knowledge and information can simply be presented, in one form or another, or students can be required to discover it for themselves. Students can encounter knowledge through 'big ideas' and 'abstract concepts' or they can encounter that same knowledge through a curriculum pathway that is personally meaningful, beginning with a concrete place, object or problem.

Now that there is so much rapidly changing knowledge out there and the answers to most questions are available on the internet anyway, the process of learning and encountering appropriate and meaningful knowledge for oneself becomes a critical educational issue.

The tension between the specialised knowledge content of the curriculum and a broader, more integrated approach is one which is likely to be present for some time yet. There are some exciting whole-school initiatives underway, such as the Opening Minds project of the RSA[3] and others, but for much of the curriculum teachers will be constrained by the boundaries of the subjects and their assessment practices. Within this framework it is still possible to teach the same things differently.

In developing a 'learning power friendly' curriculum teachers have re-organised the ways in which they presented the material for a lesson, creating a situation where students are challenged to make sense of data, and to make meaning from it. Teachers also explicitly relate the content of lessons to students' experiences outside of school and in the community, and 'scaffold' learning by inviting students to make connections with other aspects of the curriculum and with their wider life experience.

In an English classroom, rather than present the poetry and give the students the themes with which to analyse the poems, Annie set the students up to identify the themes and problems for themselves. Rather than beginning with the injustice of the slave trade in history, the teacher began with the students' own experiences of injustice in contemporary society. Problematising the material content of the curriculum is the key – knowledge is there to be uncovered and encountered rather than simply imparted or repeated.

In a primary classroom there is more flexibility. Mary tried to give coherence to a disjointed curriculum by scaffolding learning across the week, to maximise opportunities for students to make connections in their learning between, within and across subjects and inside and outside of the classroom. This meant extending some lessons, shortening others and encouraging meaning making by taking whole or half days on particular curriculum themes. For example, they would consolidate and support the learning of historical themes through art, ICT, geography, music and drama. This created more time for reflection and for the reinforcement of ideas. She also set up real-life situations, such as writing letters and going out to post them, planning and giving whole-class performances for music, engaging whole heartedly with 'cake days' through writing letters and deciding how the money raised should be spent. The aim was to enable students to see that learning in school can be meaningful and have an impact on – and be affected by – 'real life'.

These were the key themes that emerged from the research, which were apparent in every classroom where teachers were organising their teaching around learning itself. There are many other tools, strategies, approaches and techniques which support this framework that are readily available from national strategies and other professional contexts. These themes are simply headlines from the research which represent some of the key elements of learner-centred classrooms.

Summary

In this chapter we have explored how learning power operates within a complex web of relationships, values and practices in the classroom. We have:

- looked at and interpreted a whole-class learning power profile
- considered how that data can be used diagnostically to inform teaching strategies
- examined the key themes that have emerged from the research which are present in classrooms where teachers focus on developing their students' learning power. These themes are:

  - teachers' learner-centred vision and values
  - relationships characterised by trust, affirmation and challenge
  - developing a language for learning
  - using metaphors
  - modelling and imitation
  - learning dialogues
  - time for reflection
  - self-assessment
  - student choice
  - resequencing the content of the curriculum.

More examples of how these themes have emerged in primary and secondary classrooms can be found in Chapters 5–8.

 ## NOTES AND FURTHER READING

1. Bond, T. (2004) *Ethical Guidelines for Researching Counselling and Psychotherapy*. Rugby: British Association for Counselling and Psychotherapy.
2. For more on this, see Lakoff, G. and Johnson, M. (1980) *Metaphors We Live By. Chicago*, IL: University of Chicago Press.
3. RSA (2005) *Opening Minds: Giving Young People a Better Chance*. London: Royal Society for the Encouragement of Arts, Manufactures & Commerce.

Chapter 5

It's all about values: learning power and well-being

In this chapter we explore the links between learning power and personal development and well-being. We see that the values, attitudes and dispositions of learning power also have an impact on behaviour and provide a framework for the spiritual, moral, social and cultural development of students. Learning power also helps to achieve the outcomes for 'Every Child Matters'.

Developing learning power is about:

- taking responsibility for my own growth
- learning to respect other people's learning and growth
- valuing myself and valuing others
- making a positive contribution.

If we unpack learning power and begin to explore some of the key ideas, we find that learning and changing over time is something that human beings do naturally, rather like breathing. If we took a child to the doctor and said that she isn't breathing, then it would be a medical emergency. We sometimes say that children aren't learning – and this is never true! They just aren't learning the kinds of things we think they should learn and in the way we think they should learn them. At the core of the ideas developed in this book is the notion of encouraging learners to take responsibility for themselves, for their behaviour, for their aspirations and for reaching their goals. It's about valuing learners and valuing learning.

There are some very basic human needs which have to be addressed before students in schools can fully take responsibility for themselves. Students arrive in the classroom with hugely varying amounts of the sorts of social capital necessary for positive school-based learning. Being healthy and safe, for example, is fundamental. If a student does not feel safe from bullying, or safe from being put down or from abuse, then naturally he will attend to getting those needs met first. Students also need to feel valued – by their families, their teachers and their peers. When individuals do not feel valued at home, by their parents and brothers and sisters, then their efforts to feel valued by teachers or friends in school may actually produce the opposite effect – they may become labelled as an attention-seeker or a trouble-maker. These are ways of getting recognised and valued, albeit negative ways.

The values of the classroom and school are really important – and those that are spoken about need to be consistent with those that are felt. Values are hard to measure but easy to recognise in practice. Positive values – and there are a handful of core values that regularly emerge as important in most communities – are an important form of social capital. In schools, values are as vital for success as the strategies and targets of the National Curriculum.

Here, for example, are the values that the students, teachers and parents in a primary school consider to be most important in their community:

- Love of learning
- Responsibility for learning
- Respect
- Trust
- Justice
- Forgiveness.

Andrew, the head teacher, explains that these values shape the 'how' of learning and teaching. They are not imposed by any external authority – rather the students, parents and teachers identified them through a consultation process. They are the other side of the coin of learning power. Let's use Table 5.1 to look at them more closely in relation to the dimensions of learning power.

The following story is a true one and it is an example of how the values in the classroom, the behaviour of the students and learning power are all deeply related to each other.

MANDY'S STORY

Mandy was the head teacher of an inner city primary school. She was learner-centred in her leadership and the school's learning framework included many of the themes discussed in these pages. Her teachers focused on being learner-centred through creating a positive climate for learning, developing higher order creative and critical thinking skills, dialogue, respecting differing learning styles and other well-validated learner-centred themes.

One particular class of eleven-year-olds proved a particular challenge. Mandy described them in the following way:

- They are individually wonderful children – as a group they were boorish, apathetic and irresponsible.
- 41 per cent were on the Special Educational Needs register.
- Eight of the children have been excluded from other schools.
- One child was seriously under-attaining.
- Two-thirds of the class were boys.
- There were six able students in the class who were long suffering, fed up and remote.
- Apathy was the name of the game.

Table 5.1	Values and learning power
Love of learning	Enjoying learning and achievement and celebrating success. Knowing that I can learn and get better at learning.
Responsibility for learning	Self-awareness, ownership and responsibility through self-assessment.
Respect	Respecting myself as a learner – learning to listen to others, through dialogue. Learning to learn with and from others.
Trust	Trusting myself to be able to learn and trusting others to respect me so that I feel safe enough to take risks to be creative and to grow through my learning.
Justice	Being fair to myself, and to other learners. Allowing other learners to learn and teachers to teach. Knowing that fairness will prevail when things get tough.
Forgiveness	Learning to make mistakes, to fail and to know that I am still OK. Allowing other people to make mistakes and get it wrong and knowing that they are still OK.

- Two of the children had weekly in-school counselling – three more were on the waiting list!
- 'Street Cred' ruled and 'sticking with the crowd' was a big issue.
- The class kept themselves in control for teachers and adults they rated, and were totally dismissive of any unknown or un-rated adult.

Mandy, and her class teacher Jane, decided to make a concerted effort to change the climate in this very disengaged class … after all there was nowhere to go but up. They wanted to see a shift from students who were disinterested, rude and unmotivated to students who were engaged, enthusiastic and self-motivated. They wanted to shift from a climate of fear and passivity to a climate of trust, engagement and pride.

I am going to try and be an individual instead of following the crowd (Sam)

21 Jan   When Mrs M was here I was not laughing and I wasn't when everyone else was.

24 Jan   In PE when other people were being stupid I hesitated.

6 Feb   In maths I carried on with my work and ignored somebody that was talking to me.

I want to think about the questions I ask and ask them at the right time (Dan)

I have tried all week and proved it when answering a question at the wrong time and I realised and my hand shot down. I try to but I can't. I've got to not speak over the teacher's voice. I have waited recently for the teacher to stop speaking (Whooa!).

This was a rather tall order … their talented and experienced Year 6 teacher was at her wits' end and already two of the youngsters were in trouble with the law. They decided to get a single message across to these students: 'you have to power to change yourself!'

They began a class discussion about learning power and asked the students to rate themselves on a scale of 1–5 for each of the learning power dimensions. They developed their own language for each of the dimensions and displayed these around the classroom (see Figure 5.1).

Gradually the students began to get the message and set targets for themselves. Their targets were realistic, and all about behaviour. It's as though these youngsters knew that before they could achieve anything they had to sort out their behaviour.

Here Sam is aiming to be an individual – he has identified 'learning relationships' as important for him. At the same time, Dan is aiming to learn to ask appropriate questions at appropriate times as a first step towards developing his critical curiosity.

These targets and the language of learning became part of the fabric of the classroom over the year and students began to realise they could take control of their own learning and get more satisfaction that way too. The teacher spent time with the class each day reflecting on how they were doing and the positive difference it was making. The teacher's evaluation of the work at the end of the year showed that this 'embedding and living' the values of learning, talking about learning and specific learning targets on a regular basis across the curriculum, were critical success factors.

The climate of the class had changed dramatically – they had become co-operative, begun to listen to each other and their work had begun to improve. At the end of the year Mandy and Jane conducted an evaluation of the year's work with the students, focusing particularly on how the students had become better learners.

Firstly the class were asked to write down the things they had got better at over the year and the reasons for this. Their responses speak for themselves:

- I used to feel I had to stick with the crowd and copy everyone else, but now I go my own way and show out a bit more.
- … looking deeply into things, because before I just skipped a question, now I spend time on it.
- I like trying things out; last term or whatever I wouldn't try anything.
- … sticking at my work because it got hard at times but now I really try and before I would get in a mood, and I asked questions of Miss and my partner.

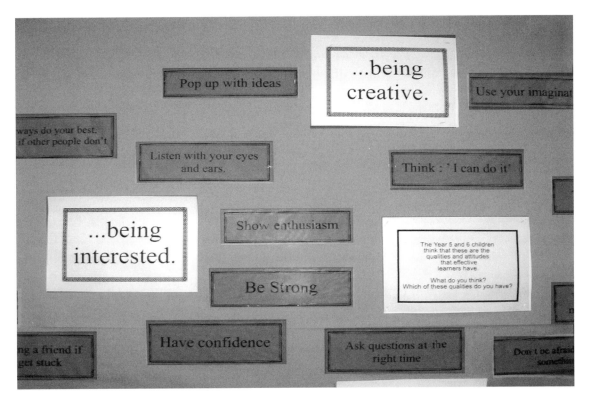

Figure 5.1   Developing a local language for learning

- I think how to plan things through now because before I asked people to help or to do if for me, now I do it for myself.
- I like to ask questions: I know this because I used never to ask questions but now I really like asking questions.

These responses show that the students had understood and internalised the ideas of learning power, and they demonstrate strategic awareness of how and why they have changed over time. You can see how each of these responses actually describes behaviour as well as showing evidence of thinking and feeling. They are about the students as people and this core work – to do with taking responsibility for themselves as learners – is foundational for both achievement and personal development. These self-evaluation statements provide evidence of the students beginning to enjoy and achieve, making a positive contribution, as well as being mentally and emotionally healthy. Without this in place there was little change of significant attainment.

However, perhaps the most interesting outcome of this year's work was the impact that it had on the students' relationships with each other. The students became much more aware of their own and other people's behaviour and instead of apathy or competition, they supported each other in the mutual change process. They were able to discuss their own and other people's personal development and change processes with insight and empathy.

Peer evaluation

C has improved in his reactions – he is learning to control his feelings, not throwing things around the table – now he hardly ever does it – it used to really bug us.

Peer evaluation

He's improved so much – he never used to say anything or show any interest and now he's amazing, he's always asking questions.

The following quotations come directly from their self-evaluation sheets in response to the question:

Do you see a difference in other people in the class?

- In class, S is always *with* the class, answering questions and discussing – she's always at the centre of the action – she doesn't get shy or sulky anymore like she did.
- G has really started to join in; he pops up with more ideas, and is more enthusiastic.
- F always used to sit like that doing nothing (slouched in chair). He used to sit like that for half an hour doing the title! – now he just gets on with it.
- H does ask as many questions, but they are now interesting ones *which help*, not just any questions all the time.
- G develops her ideas quite a lot now and is not afraid to put her hand up and work with a partner and ask questions.
- B used to moan and groan and whine 'why' and now he's completely different – he just does it.
- C used to be really quiet – she has improved more, puts up her hand and says ' I don't agree with that!'
- A has really started to ask questions – he is really interested and when we are in partners, he is really looking at me like he wants to know it, and actually helps me and give me things I didn't think of.

These examples show how the energy of learning power runs through the middle of the 'double helix of learning', which we discussed in Chapter 1. On the one hand there is attainment and the well-recognised sets of knowledge, skills and understanding that are the focus of the formal curriculum. On the other hand there is personal development, which includes the dispositions, values and attitudes necessary for life in the twenty-first century. Focusing on learning power supports both strands in critical ways and enables us to value the whole person of the learner and attend to his spiritual, emotional and social needs as well as to his intellectual development.

'EVERY CHILD MATTERS'

In England, the 'Every Child Matters' framework reflects the government's aim for every child, whatever their background or their circumstances, to have the support they need in order to:

- Be healthy
- Stay safe
- Enjoy and achieve
- Make a positive contribution
- Achieve economic well-being.

This will require co-ordination across all children's services and the framework challenges schools in new ways to attend to students as whole people and to involve them in this process through honouring student voice and participation in school self-evaluation.

The ideas and values embedded in learning power help teachers to pay attention to the needs of the whole child, while inviting students to take responsibility for their own learning and growth as whole people – including personal and social development, citizenship and academic and vocational achievement. Some of the specific issues to do with citizenship and education for enterprise will be addressed in Chapter 10. Meanwhile we will explore a bit further the ways in which taking responsibility for one's own learning links up with, and facilitates, values education and spiritual, moral, social and cultural development.

VALUES AND THE SPIRITUAL, MORAL, SOCIAL AND CULTURAL DEVELOPMENT OF STUDENTS

We have already seen how developing learning power involves attending to particular core values, and developing a language for changing and learning over time in relation to values, attitudes and dispositions – which means it is essentially about personal development as well as achievement.

In valuing learning we are valuing a process, or a journey – rather than defining a particular end point. The core values, which a community identifies as important for that journey, are rather like improvising jazz. When a jazz band plays they all understand and have experienced certain principles of rhythm, melody, harmony, and musical interaction and these principles or values shape how the music develops. They can be interpreted in different ways and the music is improvised – created at the time. The product is shaped, but not actually defined until the musicians have got there.

Developing core values is like improvising jazz

If we unpack this a little further, we can begin to see the links between values, learning power and the spiritual, moral, social and cultural development of students, which schools are also required to attend to. In a relational approach to learning, the learner is at the centre of the equation and the core values of relational learning have to do with 'valuing myself', 'valuing others' 'valuing learning', 'respect', 'trust' and 'truthfulness'.

By naming our values we do two things:

- We contribute to a language for learning and give 'voice' to things that matter
- We provide ourselves with a way of organising spiritual, moral, social and cultural development.

'Spirituality' has been a difficult concept in schools, because historically it has been so closely linked to organised religion. However, if we understand spirituality to be about the developing relationship of the individual in community to that which is considered to be of most worth and importance,[1] then we can see how it fits in more easily, whether or not the school has a religious foundation.

For example, Figure 5.2 shows that if we take 'valuing myself' as something of great significance in a learning community, it has many 'spin offs' which touch on spiritual, moral, social and cultural (SMSC) development as well as lifelong learning, vocation and enterprise and it relates to the five outcomes of 'Every Child Matters'. Each core value that a learning community identifies as important to them can inform the school culture and direction.

Each time a student encounters that core value in the curriculum, either formally or informally, there are opportunities for SMSC development to happen.

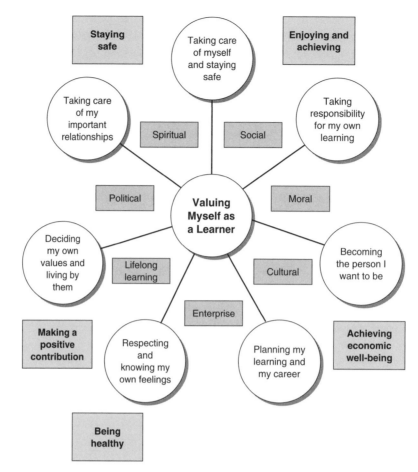

Figure 5.2   Linking values, SMSC development and 'Every Child Matters'

Core values such as these can be planned into schemes of work and lessons – they can be fore grounded as learning objectives and become part of the language of the school.[2]

Summary

We have looked more carefully in this chapter at how the energy of learning power sits in the middle of the double helix of learning power, linking attainment and personal development. In particular we saw how taking responsibility for my own learning leads to:

- changes in behaviour as well as thoughts and feelings about myself as a learner
- caring about other people and their learning
- putting the learner as a whole person at the centre of the educational equation
- understanding a set of core values that can help organise provision for spiritual, moral, social and cultural development.

NOTES AND FURTHER READING

1. Wright, A. (1998) *Spiritual Pedagogy: A Survey, Critique and Reconstruction of Contemparary Spititual Education in England and Wales*. Abingdon: Culham College Institute.
2. For more information and resources to support the development of values in the school, see the internet resource www.VitalEd.net

Chapter 6

Developing learning power in the primary classroom: animal metaphors as a vehicle for learning

David Millington

In this chapter we meet David, a primary school teacher who helps his students develop their own learning power by creating animal cartoons which embody the seven learning dimensions of learning power. These animals take on a life of their own in the classroom, providing a powerful tool for learning.

David explains:

- how the children have acquired a comprehensive understanding of the dimensions of learning power through animal cartoons and metaphors
- how the animals have helped the children in their creative writing and in problem solving
- how animal puppets have helped to promote learning power across the primary curriculum
- the impact the learning dimensions and the associated animals have had on children's development.

A REFRESHINGLY NEW APPROACH: A FOCUS ON LEARNING ITSELF

As my understanding of the seven dimensions of learning power deepened, so did my realisation that my former preoccupation with what to teach and how it should be taught was insufficient. With the seven dimensions of learning power I felt that I now had the key that for so long had kept the secrets of what makes children effective learners locked away. I knew that giving this key to my children would have a significant impact on their motivation, enjoyment of and responsibility for learning, achievement, attainment and behaviour. Moreover, by providing opportunities for the children to develop strengths in a particular learning dimension I would be able to have an impact upon the children's lives and futures in a much more meaningful and purposeful way than simply helping them to pass tests.

INTRODUCING THE SEVEN DIMENSIONS OF POWERFUL LEARNING THROUGH ANIMAL CARTOONS

If the children in my class were going to develop their learning power, I knew that it would be essential that they must first acquire a comprehensive understanding of each of the learning power dimensions. They would need to be able to identify which of the dimensions they would need to 'be powerful in' and focused upon when presented with particular learning challenges. Once they had developed a vocabulary of learning, the children would gain the confidence to reflect on their own learning or that of others in relation to each of the dimensions. Through reflection and dialogue they would then be able to identify their learning strengths and areas for development.

There are very few children of a primary age who aren't excited and intrigued by the wonders of the animal kingdom. Associating an animal with a particular dimension of learning power seemed to be a very powerful way of encouraging the children to become enthused about learning and to help them form concrete images in their minds of what powerful learners look like in terms of:

- the way they learn
- their learning skills
- their attitudes to learning.

Following a class brainstorm on 'What makes an effective learner?' I introduced the seven dimensions of learning power. The children were then divided into small groups and each allocated a learning dimension with which they had to associate an animal and justify their reasoning. Having already researched a range of African animals at home in preparation for writing poetry, the children were able to draw upon a wealth of knowledge about the characteristics and behaviours of these animals and connect them to a learning dimension:

> **Meaning Making:** Soaring high in the sky, a vulture has the ability to see how things fit together like a jigsaw. From such a great height, it is able to see the big picture and make meaning of the world below.
>
> **Resilience:** A lion is often outwitted and outpaced by its prey. If it is to taste success it must be robust, resilient and determined not to give up on the challenge.
>
> **Learning Relationships:** Elephants are very kind and caring creatures. They like to stick together and help each other when in danger or presented with a challenge.

LEARNING POWER CARTOON CHARACTERS

Realising the power of cartoons to captivate children and stir their imagination, the next step was to be to personify each animal into a cartoon. This was met with great excitement by the children who had fun creating their own learning power animal cartoon characters.

The animals have become a central feature of the physical environment both in my classroom and in my everyday teaching. In the next section I will provide some examples of how we have used them in the classroom.

THE ANIMALS AND THE CLASSROOM ENVIRONMENT

Anyone who has taught children will know how important the classroom environment is in terms of its ability to educate, inspire and excite. Shortly after the creation of the learning power animal cartoons, they began to appear at various places in and around the classroom. First of all they appeared on my interactive whiteboard as a desktop background. This was followed by a large interactive wall display. Not only do the animals appear on the display explaining their learning strengths but they also engage the children by asking them questions about how they like to learn. The cartoons are provided in Figure 6.1.

Learning power place mats

Traditionally, place mats have been used in primary classrooms to enhance the learning that takes place by providing write on and rub off spaces for children's thoughts and ideas or for the display of curriculum key objectives such as multiplication facts and high and medium frequency words. While retaining some of these features, I wanted to develop a place mat that also promoted learning power and the seven learning dimensions.

The place mat shown in Figure 6.2 has each of the learning power cartoon animal characters on display. At the beginning of a new learning activity the children or a teacher can circle the character or characters they will need to be most like. This enables the children to focus their minds not just on what it is they have to do and learn, but more importantly on how they will be able to do this through their own learning power and the necessary dimensions of learning which will ultimately determine their success.

Another unique learning power feature of the place mat is the learning power reflection line. As the children come towards the end of a particular activity or even mid-way through, I will ask them how like one or more of the learning power animal characters they have been. The children respond by placing themselves, with an arrow, on the line marked 'like' at one end and 'unlike' at the opposite end (see Figure 6.3). They must then give a reason for their positioning. This has proved to be a superb tool for encouraging the children to become reflective learners and develop a sense of ownership and responsibility for their own learning. The reflection line provides every child with the opportunity to reflect on their own learning in relation to a specific dimension and consider their own strategies for developing their learning power.

Hello, I'm Camilla and my strength is in changing. I know that I can become better at learning and thinking over time and develop strengths in all the different learning dimensions. I understand the potential of my mind and its ability to grow and expand.

Hello, I'm Vinny and my learning strength is in meaning making. Soaring high up in the sky I can see how thinking and learning is like a jigsaw. I am always trying to create the big picture by looking for links between what I already know and the new things I am learning. I am able to connect what I have learnt in one lesson with another and to my life outside of school.

Hello, I'm Lenny and my learning strength is resilience. I love to challenge my thinking and learning. I don't give up easily – even when things are difficult.

Hello, I'm Gerard and my learning strength is curiosity. I love asking my own questions to find out what's really going on.

Hello, my name is Carmen and my strength is strategic awareness. I have a toolkit of strategies that I am able to use in different learning situations. I know what tool to use, how and when to use it.

Hello, I'm Marvin and my learning strength is creativity. I love playing with possibilities and using my imagination to solve problems in different ways.

Hello, my name is Elli and my learning strength is in learning relationships. I like sharing my thoughts and ideas with others and love working with my friends to solve problems.

Figure 6.1   Learning power animal cartoons

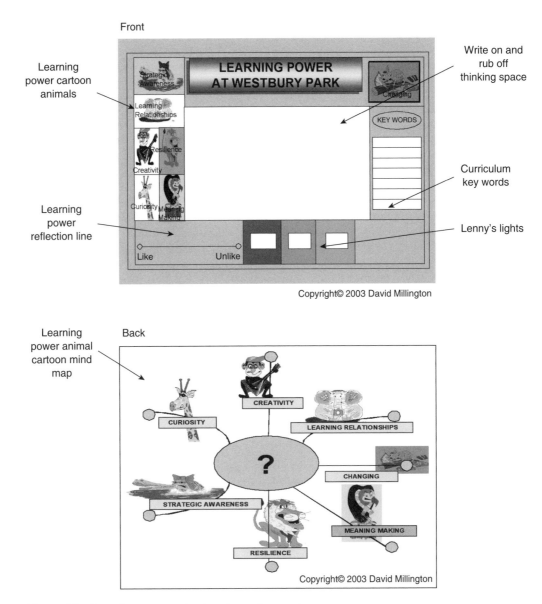

Figure 6.2   **Learning power animal cartoon place mat**

On the reverse of the place mat the learning power animals are arranged as the key branches of a mind map that can be used in a range of contexts throughout the primary curriculum. In the next part of this section I will be outlining activities which use the learning power animal cartoon mind map and which have helped children develop their own learning power through the opportunities the map provides to focus their attention on each of the learning dimensions.

Creative writing through the learning power animal cartoon mind map

The learning power animal cartoon mind map can be used as an effective tool for planning a story. This could relate to literacy units of work which require children to compose their own myths, legends, fables or other short stories of a particular genre. The starting point is to outline the main problem in a story which needs to be resolved. The following is an example of something that has worked well in my class:

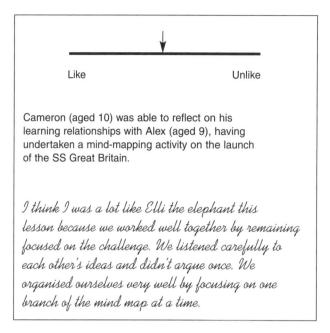

Cameron (aged 10) was able to reflect on his learning relationships with Alex (aged 9), having undertaken a mind-mapping activity on the launch of the SS Great Britain.

I think I was a lot like Elli the elephant this lesson because we worked well together by remaining focused on the challenge. We listened carefully to each other's ideas and didn't argue once. We organised ourselves very well by focusing on one branch of the mind map at a time.

Figure 6.3   Learning power animal cartoon reflection line

Story-writing stimulus: Crossing the Mara River

'You are a Masai child living in a village in Kenya. Your village elders have sent you to deliver a message to the chief of a village many miles away. On your journey you must cross the mighty Mara River. However, the only crossing point is the Mara Bridge and this has collapsed in a recent storm. How will you cross the River?'

Using the learning power cartoon mind map, the children then planned how they would cross the river by organising their thoughts and mapping their ideas in relation to each of the learning dimensions:

Key branches of the learning power animal cartoon mind map: Crossing the Mara River

Vinny the vulture/Meaning Making:
What do you need to know before, during and after crossing the river?

Marvin the monkey/Creativity:
How will you cross the river in a creative way?

Gerard the giraffe/Curiosity:
Are there any important questions you need to ask yourself?

Carmen the crocodile/Strategic Awareness:
Where will you find the resources you need to cross the river?

Lenny the lion/Resilience:
What problems will need to be overcome?

Elli the elephant/Learning Relationships:
Will you solve the problem by yourself or with the help of other characters?

Already familiar with the techniques of mind mapping, every child in the class was able to plan their stories through the dimensions which led to some highly imaginative and descriptive narratives. In one story, the Mara was crossed by the creation of a 'crocodile bridge', whereby each crocodile was linked snout to tail. In another a catapult was constructed from a nearby baobab tree. Several stories described close encounters during the crossing. The most memorable was when a herd of angry hippos which had been wallowing in the muddy banks of the river were disturbed.

Science investigations through the learning power animal cartoon mind map

The learning power animal cartoon mind map can also be used to plan and record children's scientific investigations.

Science investigation: How does exercise affect your pulse rate?

Vinny the vulture/Meaning Making:
What do you need to know before, during and after the investigation?

Marvin the monkey/Creativity:
What will you do?

Gerard the giraffe/Curiosity:
What important questions did you have to ask yourself?

Carmen the crocodile/Strategic Awareness:
What resources and methods did you use for recording your results?

Lenny the lion/Resilience:
What problems had to be overcome?

Elli the elephant/Learning Relationships:
How well did you work together?

Camilla the Chameleon/Changing and Learning:
How could you improve your investigation?

Since using the learning power animal cartoon mind map, the children have become much more successful in creating their own scientifically valid investigations, recording their observations accurately and drawing well-reasoned conclusions. Recording through the mind map has reduced the time spent on the 'not so fun' aspect of a science investigation – the write up – and has freed up time for the most enjoyable and memorable part of the investigation – experimentation and other practical aspects.

FROM CARTOONS TO PUPPETS

Following the success of the animal cartoons we made hand puppets of each of the seven animals (see Figure 6.4). When a puppet appears in a lesson, the

Learning power animal cartoon display

Gerard the giraffe hand puppet

Interactive whiteboard desktop display

Vinny the vulture hand puppet

Figure 6.4   Learning power animal cartoons and puppets on display in a classroom

children are instantly engaged in learning in a way that the human voice alone cannot achieve. Each puppet has a particular role to play in a lesson that relates to its particular learning strength. In the rest of this section I will explain how some of the puppets have been used in my teaching to help the children understand and develop further their own learning power.

Gerard the giraffe hand puppet

Gerard the giraffe's learning power is **curiosity**. He likes to learn by asking his own questions about the world in which he lives and by drawing his own conclusions. When Gerard appears in a lesson the children know that is a time for asking questions about the things they are learning. Gerard will often appear at the beginning of a lesson to introduce the key lesson objective which, through the art of ventriloquism, can be turned into a much more engaging learning question.

Gerard's learning questions

Why do we have night and day?

What do plants and animals have in common?

What makes a successful moving toy?

Why was Freddie still able to smell the perfume when he was stood so far away?

Gerard's 'Wonder Box'

Once the learning question has been introduced and the children are engaged in an activity, the children will invariably ask themselves or each other their own 'what, why, how and where' questions about the activity. These child-generated questions are the important questions from which so much learning and understanding can evolve. However, it is often the case that these important questions aren't shared, discussed or answered by the class due to the learning climate being 'knowledge centred'. To make sure these questions aren't lost, each child is given a Post-it note book at the beginning of the academic year to record their questions. Either mid-way through an activity or in the lesson plenary, Gerard appears, grabs a Post-it note by the mouth and sticks it onto an easel at the front of the class. Once again through the art of ventriloquism, questions are read aloud, and discussed by the whole class. If the question cannot be answered there and then, Gerard posts it into his Wonder Box where it is kept safe until the children have had the opportunity, either at home or school, to carry out additional research and draw their own conclusions.

Vinny the vulture hand puppet

Vinny's learning power is **meaning making**. He is able to learn by connecting information and ideas, which you can see in Figure 6.5. When Vinny appears in a lesson it is because he wants help in constructing a learning jigsaw. Having had the lesson objective introduced by Gerard and the activity outlined, Vinny picks up a jigsaw piece from inside a basket with his hooked beak. Each piece of the jigsaw has a write on/rub off space where the children can record their thoughts about what they will need to consider if they are to be successful in the activity. Once a child has recorded a thought, the jigsaw piece is displayed in a prominent position for future reference. As this is repeated the jigsaw develops until the children's ideas are exhausted or the teacher is happy that the necessary success criteria for the activity have been covered.

HOW LEARNING POWER ANIMAL CARTOON CHARACTERS AND PUPPETS HAVE MADE A DIFFERENCE TO CHILDREN'S LEARNING

The animal cartoons and puppets have been introduced across the primary age range in school. The puppets were an instant hit when I first introduced them to the infants. They have since become role models for the children and are now each enjoying a celebrity status! They have helped to engage the children in a language of learning and develop their understanding of what it is to be an effective learner. When Gerard appeared for the first time in the Year 1 class and it was explained that the thing Gerard liked to do most of all was to ask questions, Ollie (aged 5) immediately thrust her arm upwards so that she could ask Gerard a question:

Figure 6.5 Vinny's learning power jigsaw: Children's thoughts about what would help make a successful persuasive letter on an emotive issue

What do you use those funny looking tentacle things on your head for?

Delighted by her sense of wonder, I asked Ollie to see if she could find out the answer and share this with the class the next time I visited. This she did with great enthusiasm and pride:

The tentacles are actually horns. They are bigger on the male's head and are used to fight each other.

Verses from 'The Rhythm of Learning'

My name is Vinny the vulture
High in the sky I'm king
I see the world like a jigsaw
Meaning making is my thing

My name is Carmen crocodile
I'm strategically aware
I've got a toolkit of strategies
Solving problems everywhere

Further up the school, both the cartoons and the puppets have helped the children in their understanding of what it is to be an effective learner and develop their own language of learning. The creation of a song, 'The Rhythm of Learning', by children in Year 5 is just one example of this (see Appendix 1 for the full version of this song, which can be sung to a tune of your choice). Within each verse an animal is introduced and its learning power is explained. The song is now fondly sung at the beginning of each new term by the whole school.

The animal cartoons and puppets have also helped the children to become reflective learners and be more confident in sharing their learning experiences such as the problems they have faced, the strategies they have used and how successfully they were able to work with others. Through this reflective learning the children have been on a journey of discovery, alongside the learning power animals. They have found out for themselves their individual learning strengths and areas for development. Above all, the animal cartoons and puppets have helped to make learning a much more enjoyable and memorable experience.

Summary

In this chapter we heard how David has created animal puppets which embody the characteristics of learning power and appear in the classroom and throughout the school as 'facilitators of learning' in their own right.

We have looked at:

- how animal puppets can create a space for children's imagination to help them develop their own learning power
- how reflection lines and mind maps can be strategies for self-assessment
- how mind mapping, using the seven dimensions of learning power, can be used powerfully, in problem solving
- how the whole-school culture can be supported through imagination and creativity.

Chapter 7

Powerful learning in the primary school

Marcelo Staricoff

Now we meet David's colleague, Marcelo, who explains how their primary school has integrated learning power as part of their whole-school approach to learning and values.

Marcelo explains how:

- learning power fits within a whole-school vision and mission
- learning power underpins a personalised curriculum and a community of enquiry
- learning power can form part of lesson objectives and evaluations
- learning power mind maps and concept lines are tools for powerful learning.

WHOLE-SCHOOL VISION AND VALUES

Our school has always had a strong vision and core values, and we have had the opportunity to focus on and implement a range of new initiatives around values and learning which have enriched provision for teachers and students. We have seen a remarkable symbiosis between our six major areas of concern: namely Learning Power, Thinking Skills, Values, Entitlements, Philosophy and Accelerated Learning. These themes were embedded in the jigsaw of the school's development plan. They have now become fully integrated into all aspects of school life, and represent a common, learner-centred language through which we deliver the National Curriculum and through which we discuss the teaching and learning process with each other and with the children. Our approach has been captured in the 'Westbury Park Hexagon' shown in Figure 7.1.

The success of our approach comes from the willingness of teachers to transform not *what* they teach but *how* they teach. We believe that by offering opportunities to all, and enriching our classrooms with an open-ended, questioning, respectful and reflective environment we encourage the children to experiment and build up a variety of tools which they can use to direct their own learning. We are providing an experience of school as a place where the curriculum is there to be explored, and where learners can be challenged and encouraged to be self-motivated.

It's not so much about WHAT you teach as about HOW you teach it!

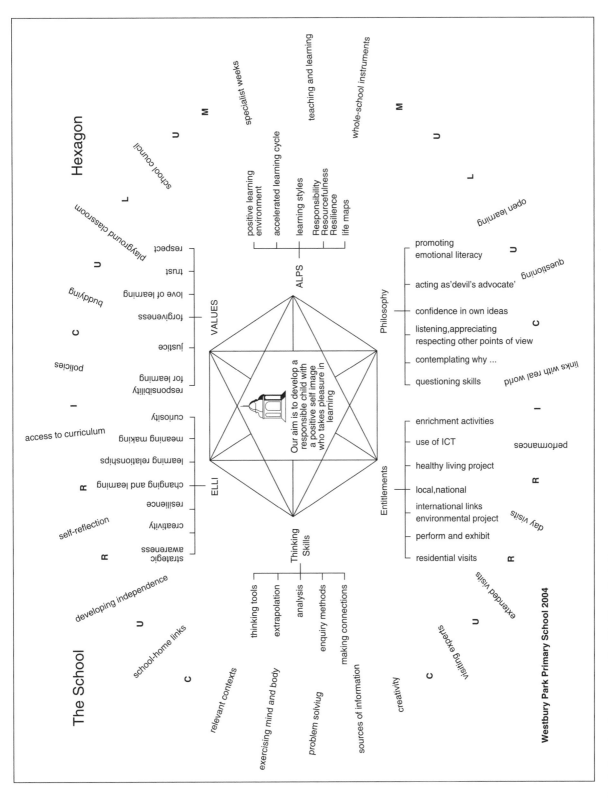

Figure 7.1 A whole-school approach: the Westbury Park Hexagon

In this way we are developing children with a positive self-image and a natural love for learning – qualities which lie at the heart of our school's core purpose statement. These values, attitudes and dispositions form an important part of the foundations on which children can build to become effective lifelong learners.

LEARNING POWER AND A LEARNER-CENTRED ENVIRONMENT

It all begins with a classroom environment that is conducive to learning and into which the children enter filled with enthusiasm and excitement for the day, week, term or year ahead of them.

The first meeting with a new class provides the perfect opportunity to discuss the learner-centred approach to the curriculum, ensuring that the ideas, language, concepts and methodology of the approach are then engrained within the constitution and expectations of a child. Being learner centred thus becomes second nature, not just among children but also teachers, learning support assistants and very importantly with parents and carers who are then able to converse with and reinforce the ideas and the language at home.

Powerful learning is now the vehicle I use to enthuse and inspire my new class. When we meet for the first time, we just chat about the concept of learning power, dissecting and analysing each of the seven dimensions and the associated animals in turn, using the discussion to formulate class definitions for each learning power dimension. These are then shared, discussed, questioned and placed in the context of each child's individual strengths and needs. In this way, I feel I'm able to inspire each new cohort and give them confidence that they will not only become more knowledgeable about the world we live in, but also feel that the dimensions of learning power will help them to face the challenges ahead with a positive attitude, whether these may be academic, social or emotional.

THREE VITAL INGREDIENTS

The seven dimensions of *learning power* make learning very explicit and help to create a *personalised learning environment* which when combined lead to the classroom as a *community of enquiry*. These are the three vital ingredients that help children feel free to question and discuss what they are learning and give them the freedom to pursue learning in their own way. It is fascinating to discuss and define the learning power dimensions with the children, to see how they assess themselves in relation to each one. We also discuss the ways in which they can strengthen themselves in different dimensions of learning power, and how this may vary across the curriculum areas. Being learner-centred enables me to describe learning as a journey on which we are all travelling and which offers endless moments of challenge and satisfaction. When we are faced with a problem we now know

Learning power

Personalised learning

Community of enquiry

what to do about it. Once the dimensions of learning power have been discussed, their definitions agreed, and each child is aware of appropriate success criteria, I feel ready to begin.

LEARNING POWER AND THE PERSONALISED CURRICULUM

Giving children the opportunity to have a say in the way that the teaching and learning cycle is conducted in the classroom is of paramount importance in the development of children's learning power. Having a common concept of what an effective learner looks like and a common language to discuss how best each child can aspire towards this goal allows us to create a classroom that functions through and thrives from discussion, enquiry, critical thinking and questioning.

TODAY'S LEARNING POINT

The powerful learning approach to the curriculum has as a basis a number of routines aimed at making the children feel comfortable and secure. All our written work is preceded by the date, the title and the lesson objective, known as the TLP – Today's Learning Point. The TLP is generated with the children and takes the form of a question. This is the most important part of our lessons and is a fantastic opportunity to develop children's curiosity and their ability for meaning making. We clarify what we are aspiring to in each lesson and how it relates to and builds upon our previous knowledge. Success criteria are then discussed and negotiated as a whole class, ensuring that everyone feels able to succeed. At this point we discuss which learning power dimensions are going to help us the most.

Once the work is completed the children add a TIL (Today I Learned) statement at the end of their work, which gives them the opportunity to reflect upon their learning and upon themselves as learners. They describe how the dimensions of learning power have helped them to achieve their success criteria or, if they have encountered difficulties, how they helped them to turn those difficulties into learning opportunities.

ENRICHMENT OPPORTUNITIES

All lessons are accompanied by an enrichment opportunity which takes the form of an open-ended, 'thinking skills'-based task designed to motivate the children by exposing them to situations where they are required to apply the TLP of the lesson in a different context. This is usually linked to a real-life scenario, or the children act as 'Teachers' to explain the concept to a peer.

Both of these avenues for enrichment provide children with a concrete model of how the dimensions of learning power can be applied to new, out-of-school context challenges that mimic real life. They enable learners to bridge the gap between school and the outside world and also allow them to relate what they learn in school to the context of their lives and personal experiences.

robotic		strategically aware
rule bound		creative
passive		curious
fragmented		meaning making
dependent		effective partner
fragile		resilient

Figure 7.2   Learning power concept lines

LEARNING POWER CONCEPT LINES AND MIND MAPS

Concept lines and mind maps[1] are invaluable tools which enable learners to unravel, disentangle, order and structure their thinking. This is essential if children are going to become successful lifelong learners.

Concept lines are lines which represent a continuum and have opposite attributes at either end. They are excellent vehicles for taking away the worry of being right or wrong and for allowing personal opinions and feelings to be expressed. As long as the children are able to justify why they have placed their character, thought, feeling or opinion in a particular place on the line, it represents their individual perception and as such cannot be judged or perceived to be wrong. Plotting themselves on learning power concept lines before and after a lesson, topic, term or year, justifying where they position themselves as learners and any movement which has occurred or that they are hoping will occur, gives children a tremendous amount of confidence and develops their responsibility for their own learning. It moves them way beyond rote learning and memorisation. You will notice that the dimension of Changing and Learning is missing from the learning power concept line in Figure 7.2 – that is because what the learner is DOING in filling in the concept line IS changing and learning.

Learning power mind maps

Through mind mapping the children are able to organise their thinking about a topic, a person, a place, or a concept in a visual way, which invariably leads them to make connections that they wouldn't have otherwise made. David and I developed the learning power mind map, where the area of focus is left blank in the middle, from which emanate the main branches, each one representing a different learning power dimension. This generic approach to problem solving has completely revolutionised our approach to thinking about and recording the outcomes of tasks from all areas of the curriculum. Here are some more examples of how we have used mind maps for powerful learning.

◉ Learning power mind map for problem solving

Copyright© 2003 David Millington

With the aid of the mind maps, the children approach problem solving with a much more positive, optimistic and enthusiastic frame of mind. Problem solving is now seen as an opportunity to combine systematic thinking with an ability to work collaboratively, developing their learning relationships, in order to achieve the desirable outcome. Using the three core subjects as examples, it is interesting to see how the learning power mind map is having such a positive impact on the children's attitude towards learning:

Maths investigations

Our weekly Maths Investigation sessions are designed to encourage children to enjoy playing with mathematical concepts, reinforcing the learning that has been accrued during the week and allowing the children to make links between maths at school with the mathematical world we live in. These are the only sessions where they are completely free to choose who they work with as long as they work in groups of three or four. We recently asked them to find out how much money the Clifton Suspension Bridge makes in a year and suggested they placed the dimensions mind map in the centre of a large piece of paper. They wrote the problem in the middle of the mind map and then began to develop each of the branches either to state what they knew or ask questions of what they needed to know and state how best to find out. The results were outstanding – the dimensions were instrumental in making the children think about the steps they needed to follow in order to make an intelligent estimation. One group came extremely close with the amount they worked out, which we confirmed by telephoning the company that runs the bridge!

> How much money does the Clifton Suspension bridge make in a year?
>
> Use the learning power mind map ...

Science investigations

As a former scientist I have always felt that the writing up of the experiment, although a very important process, tended to spoil the excitement of what one was trying to do. This is even more the case in primary education where I feel we have got the luxury of being able to present science as a subject that thrives on creativity, curiosity, meaning making, hypothesising and experimenting without having to *worry* about having to then *write it all up*. The powerful learning mind map overcomes this problem perfectly – once the task has been discussed and explained the children use the mind map as their working tool; once the activity is finished their thoughts, observations, results and next steps are all added onto the appropriate branch, and the children are able to think through the process they have engaged in rather than engage in a recollection of facts exercise.

Creative writing

Creative writing has also benefited tremendously through the powerful learning mind map and we have found that now that the children are planning their writing using the mind map, the characters are more multi-dimensional, the plots much more interesting, the climaxes much more gripping and the resolutions much more original. Again the mind map is allowing children to structure their thinking and to sequence events in a way which makes their writing clearer and more interesting and enjoyable for the reader.

ELLI AND THE PERSONALISED EXTRA-CURRICULUM

Our school's learning journey has been made particularly exciting by our innovative and experimental head teacher. He has encouraged us to take risks and to incorporate initiatives into our routine which we are passionate about, but which may not necessarily be within the realm of what is prescribed by the National Curriculum. Alan realises that what we teach can only make an impact if we also focus on *how* we teach it. He has encouraged us to be powerful learners as professionals!

Nothing illustrates this better than the daily exposure to a Thinking Skills Starter[2] or the hourly sessions that we devote to philosophical enquiry. Every morning, as the children enter the classroom, they are greeted by a Thinking Skills Starter which they engage in while the register is being taken and classical music is playing in the background. The Starters are designed to be open-ended and to promote the powerful learning approach. We have noticed that when the children share the outcomes of these and are asked to reflect upon which dimensions they feel they are nurturing through the Starters, they invariably focus on Resilience, Creativity and Meaning Making. Starters have transformed the way the children feel about school and the learning process, the enthusiasm with which they enter the classroom. Having engaged in the Starters the children then describe a feeling of 'being ready to tackle the day ahead of them'.

> Thinking Skills Starters help children 'get ready to tackle the day ahead'...

LEARNING POWER AND PHILOSOPHY

Philosophy sessions have built a very unique relationship with learning power dimensions and they occupy a very special space in our weekly timetable. Through philosophical enquiry, we are creating a classroom environment that enables us to foster children's natural tendency to be curious, to wonder, to question and to converse about the world we live in as a way of making sense of their role in society and of life in general. With philosophy, the children are aware that all the learning power dimensions come into play. Table 7.1 provides some examples.

Philosophy sessions generate a very unique classroom atmosphere and produce an immense range of thought, reasoning and original ways of looking at

Table 7.1	Learning power and philosophy
Posing interesting questions	**Critical Curiosity**
Developing the skill to listen to and use each other's ideas to develop an argument in depth	**Learning Relationships**
Being prepared to have one's mind changed during the discussion	**Changing and Learning**
Having to pursue a line of argument to convince others of a particular point of view and having to present this argument from different angles	**Resilience, Creativity**
Transferring the discussion to a new environment and becoming the propagator or facilitator for a whole new group of people to enjoy, usually their family at home	**Meaning Making, Strategic Awareness**
Deciphering how the concepts discussed and the consequences which may arise as a result of the choices being made relate to our everyday lives	**Meaning Making, Strategic Awareness**

Critical Curiosity

I nominate Isaac Newton because he was curious when he saw an apple fall from a tree and thought 'Why did that apple fall?' That's how he discovered gravity. Thinking 'why did the apple fall?' was very curious

the world around us. The children are placed in positions that require moral judgements to be made, problems to be solved and consequences to be considered, of hypothetical situations of which they may have no prior experience of. Children come in with suggestions for discussions – philosophy is a unique motivator, equipping children with the attributes that will enable them to become successful lifelong learners and critical thinkers. It also highlights the importance of values, helping enormously to develop their speaking and listening skills and self-esteem.

LEARNING POWER AT HOME AND AT SCHOOL

In order to foster the parent–child–school relationship, we have developed a learning power based approach to

Learning Relationships

I nominate the British rowing team because they all had to work together to make the boat move quickly and smoothly. This shows that they have a good learning relationship with each other.

Meaning Making

I nominate Lemony Snicket because in his books he always writes about things and then links them up with something that has happened to him. I think this makes people able to imagine what the children in the books feel like because he turns them into real-life situations.

homework. The approach is based upon open-ended tasks, connected to something that is happening in the curriculum that week. This might be a mind map of themselves, a mathematical 'odd one out' grid, a philosophical discussion, a poster advertising their favourite film, an autobiography of a person from the Victorian times, a survey of why people read fiction, a collection of as many different types of maps as possible, and so on.

The one that has provided the most wonderful amount of original thought, dedication, parental involvement and enjoyment, however, has been the one based on the learning power dimensions. In this one, the children are asked to take each dimension in turn and to choose a famous person that to them best illustrates a particular strength in that dimension, stating the reason for their choice. It is such a fantastic way of illustrating to the children and parents what we mean by each learning power dimension and how success in a particular field almost demands one to be very strong in at least one dimension.

Some children choose a person and in their justification explain that although they are particularly strong in a certain dimension, their success could not have been achieved had they not been strong in some of the others too. This is a truly fantastic way to bring the dimensions alive and provides a fascinating insight into children's and parent's personal interests – unique insights which can then be cultivated in the classroom and enrich the life of all of us.

The thinking skills home learning books become very precious to them and the dedication shown is always admirable. Children with particular gifts, talents or interests have amazed us time and time again by producing thinking and material of unimaginable originality and quality of presentation – often way beyond the highest expectations that one may have had for that child. Celebrating their successes completes the cycle. It has become very popular for the children to use the homework tasks to invent their own 'games' based on particular topics. These games are not only extremely professional but have also become *the* games the children want to play in their free time. It is difficult to think of a more purposeful and meaningful way of promoting creativity, and curiosity within the classroom and at home.

Playing Improvisation Games whenever we have a spare few minutes has also contributed enormously to developing learning power, giving children the chance to shine in a fun and respectful atmosphere. These games are based on 'Whose Line is it Anyway?', or 'De Bono's Six Thinking Hats', or adapted from 'Robert Fisher's Games for Thinking'.[3] Playing with the children's ability to improvise, think on the spot and observing them doing so in front of an audience has opened many doors both for the confident ones and for the children who really pluck up the courage once, and then never look back – changing and growing in front of our eyes!

Strategic Awareness

I nominate Kelly Holmes because she has strategies and was aware that everyone else would be tired by the end so she stayed back and saved her energy until the end. This was a good strategy.

LEARNING POWER: TRANSFORMING THE NATIONAL CURRICULUM FROM A CAGE INTO A SCAFFOLD

The impact that learning power has on the curriculum transforms it from a cage, which closes learners down, to a scaffold, which opens them up to learning and living. It is having an impact on the lives of everyone involved in the school in a manner that is difficult to quantify but very easy to observe. The perceived success of this approach could be summarised the concept that Deborah Eyre[4], describes as 'Intellectual Playfulness'. Everything that I have described in this chapter and that I believe has had a such a positive impact on all children can be summed up by the fact that this approach is indeed allowing children, teachers and parents to feel involved, free of any worries and therefore able to experiment and play, but in an intellectual way. Learning power is a transformational tool which is revolutionising the way that teaching and learning is presented, perceived and experienced by children, teachers and parents, across the whole primary age range.

Summary

In this chapter we have seen how learning power can be integrated within a school's vision and mission, and can powerfully support a personalised curriculum and a community of enquiry.

We have seen how:

- learning power can inform lesson objectives
- learning power concept lines support self-assessment
- learning power mind maps can support problem solving across the curriculum.

 # NOTES AND FURTHER READING

1. Murris, K. and Haynes, J. (2000) *Storywise: Thinking Through Stories*. Newport: Dialogue Works. David and I developed the learning power mind maps and concept lines as part of our collaborative learning.

2. For more on Thinking Skills Starters, see:

    Staricoff, M. and Rees, A. (2003a) 'Thinking Skills Transform Our Days', *Teaching Thinking and Creativity*, 10, 40–3.

    Staricoff, M. and Rees, A. (2003b) 'Start the Day on a Thought', *Teaching Thinking and Creating*, 12, 40–4.

    Staricoff, M. and Rees, A. (2004) 'The Four Fours Challenge', *Teaching Thinking and Creativity*, 15, 10–14.

    Staricoff, M. and Rees, A. (2005) *Start Thinking*. Birmingham: Imaginative Minds Publishers.

    Sutcliffe, R. and Williams, S. (2000) *The Philosophy Club: An Adventure in Thinking*. Newport: Dialogue Works.

3. De Bono, E. (1985) *Six Thinking Hats*. Boston, MA: Little, Brown.

    Fisher, R. (2003) *Games for Thinking*. York: York Publishing Services.

4. Deborah Eyre is the Director of the National Academy for Gifted and Talented Youth.

Learning power in the secondary school

Tim Small

We have seen how inventive teachers can be with the ideas and strategies associated with learning power in a primary classroom and the difference this can make to every child's ability to take responsibility for their own learning. Now we meet Tim, a former secondary head teacher, who considers:

- the problems posed by a more fragmented experience of the curriculum and over-emphasis on exam performance
- how the language and concepts of learning power can help us to overcome negative factors, integrate our efforts and improve the learning ecology
- themes and principles that have emerged from research in secondary schools working with learning power
- some examples of lessons and strategies that work well.

There are several reasons why a secondary school classroom might offer a less favourable ecology for learning power than its primary counterpart.

We have already seen that learning power is about linking personal development to academic achievement: attending to the 'whole person'. Primary schools are naturally suited to this, because one teacher takes responsibility for a class for most of their learning time: for their progress in subjects and their growth as people, in a compact learning community.

The way most secondary schools are organised puts learning into many more separate boxes. At Key Stage 3, often immediately after leaving their primary school, children might have ten or more teachers, plus a tutor. The teachers may see themselves as teachers of their subjects, rather than as teachers of people. The tutor may only meet the class briefly, once or twice a day and once a week for a single lesson. Pastoral and academic matters are usually managed through different teams and lines of responsibility. Spiritual, moral, social and cultural development may be put into another box, conveying the wrong impression that these things are unconnected with learning in other subjects.

As students move through Key Stage 3 and into Key Stage 4, the impact of testing and assessment increases. We know this depresses motivation and causes negative attitudes in some students that seriously undermine

Making sense

When students can see how the learning and values in different areas of school life all hang together, they are more likely to accept responsibility for their own progress and support and learn from each other.

their learning power. The rest of the class cannot be unaffected. Since exam results are the most important outcomes a school and its students can achieve, the timetable, syllabus, lesson objectives, homework, planners, assessment and data systems, conversations and reports and even assemblies may all be geared to raising performance. The danger is in a kind of obsession, where passing tests and meeting targets become the 'be-all and end-all', without considering the students' capacity to learn. With staff responsible for 'pupil progress' as part of their own performance management, a student can receive a surfeit of target-driven messages and exhortations from teacher after teacher, each unaware of their cumulative effect. The more a student sees herself as part of an 'exam factory', the less she will feel, think and behave as a pioneer on a learning journey for which she will ultimately take full responsibility.

While none of this makes it impossible to develop learning power, it raises important questions about how learners in a secondary school can be helped to make complete sense of their experience as learners. The better they can do this, the better they can grow their own learning power. Once again, it comes down to what is valued and how those values are experienced.

All this may help to explain why learning power, as measured by ELLI, declines as people move into and through secondary school. The research suggests that there is a terrible irony going on here. Since high levels of learning power are associated with high scores in National Curriculum assessment, it seems likely that an over-emphasis on exam performance and targets brings about the opposite of the desired effect and actually hinders people from achieving their full potential.

Exams and tests are here to stay. I am not suggesting for a moment that success in them is unimportant, or subordinate to some soft-centred ideal of personal well-being for its own sake. What the ELLI research shows is that a more holistic, learner-centred approach enables students to score better in tests and exams *and* be more effective learners throughout the rest of their lives.

If we remember the two strands that run alongside each other in the double helix of learning, we can use the ideas and practices associated with learning power to help us re-balance the emphasis and re-connect parts of the secondary curriculum that may have become fragmented.

CREATING A MORE INTEGRATED WHOLE-SCHOOL ECOLOGY FOR LEARNING POWER

By introducing the language and concepts of learning power into their teaching and learning strategies, secondary schools are developing understanding of how ELLI can make most difference in this phase. Some interesting lessons have emerged.

Firstly, schools can use ELLI to highlight and develop the links between personal and academic development. School structures and processes can be re-designed to support this.

Empowering tutors to become 'learning power managers'

In one large secondary school in the south of England, the tutor's role was built up into a major part of the school's strategy for improving performance. Tutors were given enough time with their classes to get to know them all as individuals. They had pastoral responsibility but also became the 'learning managers' for their classes, receiving regular information from all the teachers about how their students were getting on and having one-to-one conversations with the students about it. Every term, the timetable was suspended for a day and the tutors conducted 'Academic Reviews', having 'surgeries' with each of the students and their parents together. Once the ELLI Profiles became available, these were used to inform the conversations on Review days. The language of learning power and its seven dimensions began to be shared and cross the boundaries between tutor and teacher and between home and school. Tutors began to ask teachers in the different subjects to take account of the needs identified in the ELLI Profiles and adapt their teaching strategies to meet those needs. The students experienced the adults in their lives all 'singing from the same hymn sheet' – and, because of the nature of the ELLI Profiles, the students' own perceptions of themselves as learners were at the centre of the dialogue and grew stronger.

Secondly, schools can 'think outside the box' and take a radical look at curriculum design. The National Curriculum was designed in the 1980s, mainly by committees of subject specialists. Since then, we have learned that the subject content does not have to be the sole organising idea for its delivery. If a school is committed to the principles of learning to learn and empowering learners, then these values can determine the way the curriculum is designed, taught and assessed.

The 'Opening Minds' Curriculum

In another secondary school, the Key Stage 3 curriculum was re-designed to put learning power 'centre stage'. As part of the RSA's 'Opening Minds' project, funded by the Lifelong Learning Foundation, this school decided to base the curriculum and its assessment on five 'competencies':

- learning to learn
- citizenship
- relating to people
- managing situations
- managing information.

Students were taught by teams of six teachers, who changed every half-term. Some teachers and students found this disruptive at first, while others found it dynamic and invigorating. Students adapted quickly because they saw each of their teachers more frequently and many commented on how nice it was to meet up again with them later in the year. The learning relationships were different and students were set very high expectations on which they thrived. At any one time a student would follow four broad themes, to ensure that the content of the National Curriculum could be covered. During Year 8, it became clear that most students were racing through the curriculum and would be able to start some subjects at GCSE in Year 9. In the end, the three-year KS3 was reviewed and the decision taken to reduce it to two years.

(Continued)

Now, the school is using ELLI to evaluate its radical approach and reinforce the message that its students are no longer passive recipients but active agents in their own learning. The concepts and language of learning power are like new 'tools' for students already used to taking responsibility for their learning. Those in Year 11, who have already completed some of their GCSEs, are working with a university professor on starting their own action enquiries, creating 'knowledge maps' and looking at what it means to become an 'expert learner'.

LEARNING POWER AND NATIONAL STRATEGIES

Teachers introduced to what seems like a brand new set of ideas have been known to mutter, darkly, 'Not another b***** initiative!' This is inevitable when we are under pressure, unless we can understand the 'new' as just another way of looking at what we are already doing: keeping the simple goal in mind – improving learning.

Primary schools have had 'Excellence and Enjoyment', following on from the Literacy and Numeracy Strategies. Secondary schools have been working with the Key Stage 3 and 14–19 Strategies for some time and are getting used to 'Personalised Learning' and 'Every Child Matters'. Reforms to the workforce and pay arrangements have occupied much time and energy.

Looking through the 'lens' of learning power and the ELLI concepts can help us to make sense of these initiatives. What could be more apt to 'Personalised Learning' than having a way of identifying individual learning needs and characteristics and devising ways of meeting them? When we look at the five desired outcomes of 'Every Child Matters' (see Table 8.1), we can easily see how the language of learning power fits in.

CREATING AN ECOLOGY FOR LEARNING POWER IN THE SECONDARY CLASSROOM

Teachers working with ELLI in secondary schools came to see that it did not ask them to teach different things, but to teach things differently.

It is worth reminding ourselves of the key themes that emerged from the research, which together created an 'ecology' in which learning power could grow best:

- Teachers' learner-centred vision and values
- Relationships characterised by trust, affirmation and challenge
- Developing a language for learning
- Using metaphors
- Modelling and imitation
- Learning dialogues
- Time for reflection
- Self-assessment
- Student choice
- Re-sequencing the content.

Table 8.1	ELLI and the Five Outcomes of the 'Every Child Matters' initiative
Being healthy Staying safe	When I value myself as growing and changing, relating well to my fellow students and adults but also OK without them, resilient in the face of difficulties and able to make meaning out of new experiences with what I already know, I am better equipped to look after myself and other people too.
Enjoying and achieving	If I am encouraged to be creative in my learning, playing with ideas and metaphors and telling my own learning story, I am going to have fun and achieve much more
Making a positive contribution	ELLI Profiles help me to value the differences and gifts of every individual; my learning power is about taking responsibility for playing my part in a learning community
Achieving economic well-being	Effective Lifelong Learning is about having the attitudes, values and enterprise to succeed with my life's future challenges and the strategic awareness to see them coming.

By keeping these in mind while planning lessons and schemes of work, it is possible to devise learning activities in which the subject curriculum is covered while students also develop and attend to their capacity to learn.

For example, Jumila was teaching English to Emma's Year 10 GCSE class. They were hard going, because they did not get on particularly well with each other and Jumila had often restricted them to individual or pair work, to avoid conflict. They were getting a bit fed up of four-part lessons, hearing about, practising and reporting back on word-level, sentence-level and text-level reading and writing skills. They were about to move on to the different purposes of writing: to inform, explain, instruct, describe, narrate and persuade. Working with ELLI had made Jumila feel that a new approach might help her to re-engage the class and 'gee them up a bit'. She knew them well enough by now to take a risk or two.

It was the second half of the summer term and Jumila remembered a writing project that she had really enjoyed when she was at school. She had produced a whole teen magazine on sugar paper when she was thirteen. She adapted the idea for her Year 10 class, getting them to work in teams as well as alone and setting them up to make choices and decisions. She knew that some of them would find it difficult, but she wanted to bring the business of their learning relationships to a head and get them to confront their weakness as a class. It happened that this year group, in which Jumila was a tutor, had been working with the seven dimensions of learning power in their tutorial sessions. The

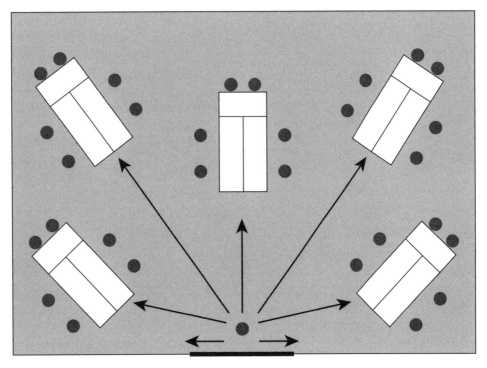

Figure 8.1   The seating plan for the six-person 'editorial boards'

more she thought about it, the more scope she could see for bringing the seven dimensions into the main focus of the lessons.

Jumila prepared for the project by organising the class into teams of six, each containing its fair share of leaders and enthusiasts and keeping the more 'challenging' students apart. She made a 'fan' formation of the tables, as shown in Figure 8.1, to enable individual, pair and team work, with spaces for her to join each group and also be seen at the board by everyone.

When the first lesson arrived, Jumila told the class that she was going to try something new with them. It would be challenging, she said, but she trusted them to make a go of it and do it well. She asked them to remember that she was learning too, and they could help her to be a better teacher by working with her in different ways. She told them frankly but kindly that she thought that they needed to get on better with each other. This would help them. She also went through all the seven dimensions of learning power again with them and asked them to be on the look out for opportunities to build them. Then she put them in their teams and gave each team a piece of A3 paper with a heading and half-formed mindmap on it. There were some ground rules underneath. The instructions asked them to start by completing the mind map together. A completed example is shown in Figure 8.2.

The energy generated by this project took Jumila by surprise. Before the end of the first lesson, she was conscious of feeling redundant in the room, as the groups ignored her, relished the chance to use their imaginations and got stuck into the decision making they had been asked to do. The choice of task was a good one, since it was easy for these fifteen-year-olds to relate it to their own experience. Some of them had stacks of back issues to bring in and raid for ideas. At first, what Jumila found herself doing most was to remind individuals to refer to their group for decisions, instead of coming to her. In time, she was able to spend more time reflecting with them on the learning processes they were engaged in and pointing out the many ways in which they were demonstrating the seven dimensions of learning power in action.

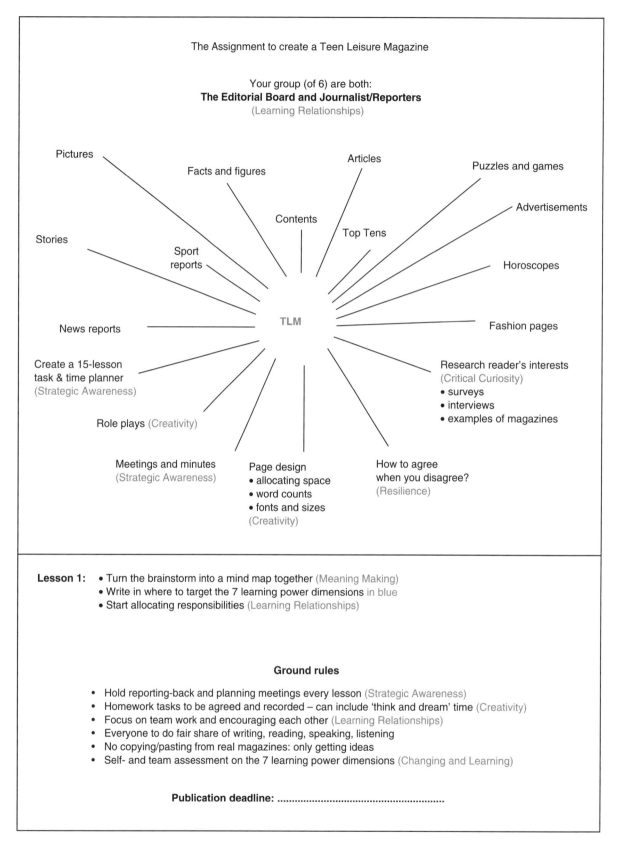

The Assignment to create a Teen Leisure Magazine

Your group (of 6) are both:
The Editorial Board and Journalist/Reporters
(Learning Relationships)

Pictures

Facts and figures

Articles

Puzzles and games

Advertisements

Contents

Top Tens

Stories

Sport
reports

Horoscopes

TLM

News reports

Fashion pages

Create a 15-lesson
task & time planner
(Strategic Awareness)

Research reader's interests
(Critical Curiosity)
• surveys
• interviews
• examples of magazines

Role plays (Creativity)

Meetings and minutes
(Strategic Awareness)

Page design
• allocating space
• word counts
• fonts and sizes
(Creativity)

How to agree
when you disagree?
(Resilience)

Lesson 1: • Turn the brainstorm into a mind map together (Meaning Making)
• Write in where to target the 7 learning power dimensions in blue
• Start allocating responsibilities (Learning Relationships)

Ground rules

• Hold reporting-back and planning meetings every lesson (Strategic Awareness)
• Homework tasks to be agreed and recorded – can include 'think and dream' time (Creativity)
• Focus on team work and encouraging each other (Learning Relationships)
• Everyone to do fair share of writing, reading, speaking, listening
• No copying/pasting from real magazines: only getting ideas
• Self- and team assessment on the 7 learning power dimensions (Changing and Learning)

Publication deadline: ....

Figure 8.2   The assigment: teen leisure magazine

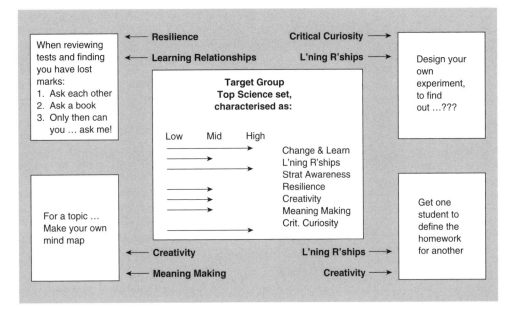

Figure 8.3 Aide-mémoire

When the writing started to come in, Jumila invited a friend of hers in publishing to come and talk to the class about proof-reading and editing. Jumila then followed this up with the groups, coaching them while they practised these essential skills. As she was doing this, she took the opportunity to explain the characteristics of different styles of writing for different purposes, using students' own work, as well as their published magazines, for examples that meant something to them. To her relief, the 'official' curriculum seemed to be covered effortlessly. In the end, Emma and most of her classmates found they had written their best piece so far for their GCSE folder, meeting the criteria because they had been writing for a purpose that they could identify with. They had each also plotted the development of their learning power on at least two of the dimensions.

LEARNING POWER IN DIFFERENT SUBJECTS

It might be said that English offers more scope than some other subjects for this kind of approach, since it is all about communication and learning *through* language as well as about it. In reality, there are opportunities in every subject to plan and build on learner-centred principles. Using the dimensions of learning power as a stimulus for their creativity, secondary subject specialists have become just as inventive and purposeful as their primary colleagues.

For example, two teachers looking at the ELLI Profiles of their very able, shared science set, found the group generally strong on changing and learning, strategic awareness and critical curiosity, but only around average at learning relationships, creativity, resilience and meaning making. They thought of four strategies that could help and created a poster for the prep-room wall, as an *aide-mémoire*. It looked like the one shown in Figure 8.3.

All too aware how easily some students give up on foreign languages, some members of a modern languages department decided to make a list of ideas for developing resilience through their teaching of a project in which students had to find new language to invent a 'perfect community':

Resilience in modern foreign language (MFL)

Rewarding small successes and visually representing progress

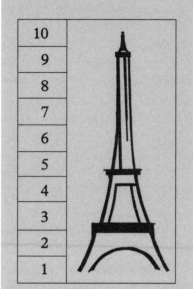

Colour in the tower to show how many new community words and phrases you have found out this week

Ideas

Flag	Map
Population	Dress
Culture	Environmental
Language	issues
Currency	Economic issues
Music	Social issues

Compare:

- LEDC (poor) countries
- MEDC (rich) countries

- Train learners how to become more independent, e.g.
  - teach dictionary skills
  - teach how to use other reference materials, e.g. verb tables, text books
- Introduce timed challenges
- To discourage weaker students from giving up too early:
  - represent progress visually
  - reward extremely small successes
- To improve confidence in speaking, aim to answer at least 1 – then 2 – then 3 question(s) each lesson
- Look for cognates to build confidence: languages are easy!
- Set 'mission impossible' tasks to build awareness that failure to complete a task is experienced by everybody and does not equal failure
- To boost confidence, move from choral repetition to small group repetition, before 'going solo'.

Richard, a geography teacher, worked in the school with the 'Opening Minds' Curriculum, described on page 80. While working with the five 'competencies', he had decided to concentrate on learning relationships with his Year 8 class. He started by dividing them into groups, as Jumila had, splitting the class into four. Each group was to prepare a presentation on its chosen topic. Four topics, each based on a different country, were available and the groups had to bid for the one they thought they could do best. The topics were:

- The UK
- Nigeria
- The Gambia
- The USA.

A list of ideas was offered as a stimulus, but Richard made it clear that these were not mandatory or exhaustive. The ground rules were quite elaborate. Groups were allowed to sub-contract work to their own members, so that individuals, pairs or smaller groups could specialise within the topic if the group agreed. After a specified time – about twenty minutes into the second lesson – the groups were asked to identify an aspect of their topic that they would appreciate help with. Members of other groups could then volunteer to leave their 'home group' for a part of the project and offer their 'learning gift' to the others.

In each of the four groups, to satisfy their 'competencies curriculum' assessments, they had to practise and assess each other's skills in managing information, in three ways:

- Finding information
- Presenting information
- Analysing information.

Managing information

- **Finding out** (facts)
- **Presenting** (speech, visual aids, powerpoint slides)
- **Analysing** (e.g. Would you want to live in that country? Explain why 'Yes!' or 'No!')

Richard's plan had deliberately and cleverly inter-meshed these three skills with a focus on learning relationships. Once the project was underway, though, he saw that most of the other learning power dimensions were also benefiting enormously from the learning processes involved. He noticed, for example, that critical curiosity was fostered by students having to ask questions in order to find out facts about their chosen country. Creativity was helped by the fluid movement of students between groups, giving them access to different ideas and perspectives. The way they were learning from others, even teaching each other how to learn, was a great example of changing and learning. When offering their 'gifts' to other groups, students showed considerable strategic awareness, having to understand and explain how their own learning strengths could be utilised by and benefit others. Lastly, in asking for help and receiving encouragement from each other, Richard could see people's confidence and resilience growing from lesson to lesson.

Maths Monkey Business

The monkey is on a log, dancing from one end to the other, rolling down a hill.

What questions might you ask, about the speed, distance and direction of his travel?

How might they be solved?

A quick glance back at the key themes is enough to see how strongly they shine through these learner-centred classrooms: the planning is founded on vision and values; relationships are attended to properly; students are valued by being challenged and given choice; metaphors like 'subcontracting', 'learning gifts' and 'mission impossible', together with the seven dimensions and five competencies, all contribute to a rich, new language for learning. By letting go a little of the role of 'subject expert', by setting open-ended tasks, allowing students to discover their own sources and sequences of knowing and to assess their own progress against shared criteria, these teachers are freeing themselves to 'learn alongside', modelling and reflecting aloud on what it means to be an 'expert learner'. Meanwhile, the learners have become responsible for decision making and problem solving that were previously done for them.

There is not room in this chapter to give practical examples for every subject in the secondary curriculum. What works far better is imaginative teachers taking and applying these principles to the contexts they know best. The last example is therefore a general one, produced by a group of teachers working with ELLI, who mapped the seven dimensions of learning power onto five familiar components of the teacher's professional environment:

- Language
- Resources
- Teaching ideas
- Measurability
- Classroom environment.

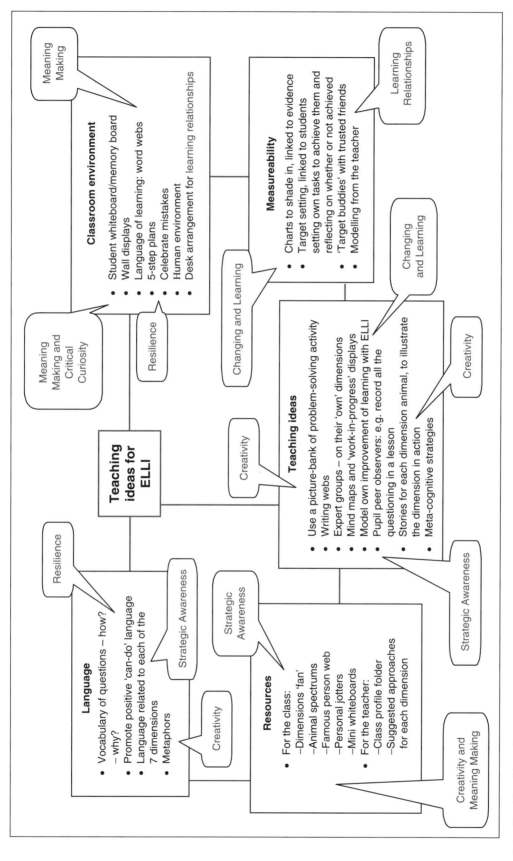

Figure 8.4 Teaching ideas for ELLI: teachers' mind map

LEARNING POWER AND THE SECONDARY SCHOOL STUDENT

We started this chapter by recognising the value of integrating our efforts in the more fragmented environment of the secondary school. We have seen what teachers, leaders and departments can do to develop a common language of learning and create learning opportunities out of the shared values and principles that this book is all about. We also need to remember that it is about helping learners to take responsibility for themselves. Ultimately, there is only one person in a position to make complete sense of the experience in all these different subject boxes: that is the student. If it is part of the school's ethos, the hope and expectation is that students will come to accept and welcome this responsibility during their secondary school years.

Learning power profiles can play a crucial part in this development. In the next chapter, we shall pick up this theme of 'emancipation' and valuing what people have to say about themselves. By supporting their students in how they approach and answer the survey questions and then interpret their own profiles, tutors are staying true to the fact that ELLI is a self-report questionnaire. By then encouraging students to develop their own strategies in response to the profile, they can gently reinforce the basic truth that we all ultimately write and craft our own life stories.

Things to try, to increase my awareness of myself as changing and learning:

- Think of yourself as a learner – the best thing to be, all life long!
- Think about how your body gets stronger and fitter with exercise and start an exercise regime for your mind and brain
- When learning is difficult – your brain 'hurts' – remember it is making your 'learning muscles' stronger
- Look at some of your old exercise books and assignments and compare what you were doing a year or more ago with what you are capable of doing now
- Keep a learning journal: record your hopes, plans, successes, failures and other milestones each week
- Think of your progress as a 'learning journey'
- Make a map of your learning journey and give yourself a reward whenever you climb 'little mountains'
- Ask your teachers to help you to notice the new things you are learning to achieve
- Remember, there are no such things as 'mistakes': only lessons to learn! Every experience moves you forward, if you want it to.

Matthew was a Sixth Form student, in Year 12 of a school that had introduced ELLI into its tutorial programme. He was already pretty good at taking responsibility for himself. He had achieved good GCSE results and felt that he had his own 'ways and routines' of studying and achieving success in examination courses. He and his friends felt a little patronised at first, when their tutor told them about a survey that could show them 'how to learn better'. They thought, at their age, they had got beyond needing to learn how to learn.

Once they had completed the survey, however, and understood their own profiles with the help of some explanation and discussion of the seven dimensions, they became more interested and wanted to know more about how these ideas could help them with their courses.

Matthew wanted to know how he could develop in the dimensions he saw he was less strong in: changing and learning and creativity. After talking and working with a teacher trained in ELLI concepts and practices, he had a list of tips and suggestions for each of these dimensions, which he typed onto cards small enough to keep in his pocket. He referred to these cards from time to time, when working on assignments at home and in study periods. He found them particularly helpful when he was 'stuck' and had feelings of being 'useless'. The changing and learning card and his new 'Journal' helped him remember that he'd overcome obstacles many times before in his learning journey, while the creativity card gave him confidence to try new ways of dealing with problems – and sometimes deciding *not* to deal with them until he had changed his routine: taking a break, giving his mind a 'breather', trusting it to come up with an answer 'when he wasn't looking'. The Learning Power Flashcards are provided in a wallet at the back of the book and are designed for learners (and their teachers!) to use for themselves. In addition, a photocopiable version of the flashcards can be found in Appendix 2.

Things to try, to increase my creativity as a learner:

- Try guessing at solutions before working them out; see how good your guess was
- Play games with routine tasks like revision, rote learning and writing up notes: e.g. timing yourself; inventing a board game; playing 'any questions?' or swapping quizzes with a friend
- Make up characters and situations in which the concepts, ideas and facts in your learning come to life for you: write or imagine scripts and scenes
- Use colour and draw pictures, diagrams, funny faces, symbols, to illustrate your notes
- Make mind maps with labels or draw 'trees' with 'meaning branches' to show how possibilities multiply when you think about alternative scenarios
- Use a different kind of writing to present your work: e.g. a stream of consciousness, diary, a cartoon, a news article; try a story book with illustrations, to explain the topic to a much younger learner
- Think about the rules you tend to follow in your learning and see if you can break them constructively by doing something differently
- Let your mind 'float free' when you are stuck or puzzled; see if your 'dreams' come up with a way forward
- Trust your subconscious mind as much as you do your thinking ability.

Summary

In this chapter, we have looked at the challenges and opportunities to be found working with learning power in the secondary school, noting in particular how:

- sharing the language and concepts of learning power can help teachers, learners, leaders and parents to connect up the different parts of the secondary school experience
- there are rich opportunities to work in this way, right across the subject-based curriculum: not by teaching different things, but by teaching them differently
- being encouraged to work with their own learning power helps young people to take fuller responsibility for their life and learning.

Chapter 9

Learning power, leadership and school self-evaluation

In this chapter we see how learning power is the fuel required for self-evaluation at all levels of the learning community. The self-evaluating school needs leaders who are committed to, and embody, the values which create a climate for changing and learning for students, teachers and the learning organisation as a whole. We explore how:

- Collecting and making meaning out of complex data and using this to inform a better future is at the heart of self-evaluation and transformative learning
- Learning power is the fuel for self-evaluation
- Leadership for learning power is values driven – values shape both the journey and the destination
- Student self-evaluation, teacher self-evaluation and organisational self-evaluation are key channels for change.

Schools which embody the values of learning are places where, at every level, people are seeking to improve the way they do things. Collecting data, making sense of it and responding intelligently is something that human beings do naturally all of the time – self-evaluation is about doing this more systematically, collaboratively and formatively. This process is part of the core purpose of a learning community. It is written into the curriculum and into the school development planning process. It is at the heart of self-evaluation – how an organisation, or a living system, becomes strategically aware of and manages its own changing and learning processes over time. Learning power is the fuel for self-evaluation.

Three characteristics of self-evaluating schools are important:

- Knowledge is seen as a process as much as a product; it is how it is managed and responded to that matter more than how well it is repeated.
- A journey of changing and learning requires a compass and a sense of direction – a transformative moral purpose.
- The social and intellectual capital of trust and truthfulness is essential to a learning culture.

KNOWLEDGE AS PROCESS AS WELL AS PRODUCT

Self-evaluating schools

Knowledge as process

Shared moral purpose

Trust and truthfulness

The ability to select relevant data, make meaning from it and integrate it with other data for a particular purpose is a far more sophisticated and desirable skill for today than simply being able to memorise and repeat information in order to pass tests or to meet performance targets. On the other hand there are particular core disciplines where a rigorous accumulation of increasingly complex ideas, such as maths or literacy, is a very necessary foundation for knowledge manipulation. Finding the balance between these two necessary processes is an outstanding problem for schooling today which profoundly challenges our current assessment practices.

Meanwhile 'knowledge as process' is critical for self-evaluation, for leaders, teachers and students. A pathway through a curriculum is much more meaningful to a learner (whether a teacher or student) when it begins with real life and experience and then involves digging deeper for more information, explanation and the acquisition of relevant skills. There are rarely set answers and, for self-evaluating students, teachers and organisations, the skills and processes of enquiry must become as natural as breathing.

TRANSFORMATIVE MORAL PURPOSE

Schools could be very effective learning communities and yet be working in a direction that does not serve the values of humanity. Some of the world's most notorious human rights atrocities have been committed by highly educated people.[1] Learning requires a direction and a moral purpose. It should include a dialogue with the values of humanity. Whenever learning addresses real-life issues and experience students will encounter questions of values. These can be foregrounded – as an intrinsic part of the enquiry – or ignored. Issues like sustainability, social justice, truthfulness and the value of human life are part of the fabric of learning and personal development. Schools can tap into the particular cultural and religious traditions of their communities in order to draw upon the necessary resources for this important element of lifelong learning. Schools must be clear about their moral purpose – and a set of shared values, owned by the community, drawing on its traditions, is a powerful educational tool. It's not about imposing values and beliefs – it's about a critical dialogue with a particular community's values and traditions, comparing and critiquing these against the core values of humanity.

SOCIAL CAPITAL OF TRUST AND TRUTHFULNESS

We have seen in Chapter 5 how values are integral to learner-centred communities. Trust and truthfulness are particularly important. If self-evaluation is taken seriously, then no one person is likely to be absolutely right, or have the answers ahead of time. Relationships which are respectful and trusting, where mistakes are accepted as part of learning and where collaboration is the norm, form the infrastructure of the learning community as a living system. Risk, uncertainty, difference and inequality are all challenges of living, learning systems – trust is a form of social capital, hard to measure but easy to 'feel', which has to be engendered by leaders and shared by all members. Building trust requires leaders who are trustworthy and this implies that learning professionals must attend as much to their inner integrity and identity as to their external skills and professional activities.

Truthfulness on the other hand is about a personal and professional commitment to that which is true and worthwhile, and fulfils the learning community's shared (and articulated) moral purpose. Modern society has depended on 'hard facts' and the scientific method to judge what is 'true'. Important though a rigorous and scientific approach to school improvement is, there are important elements of humanity and of a learning community that cannot easily be measured.

DIFFERENT WAYS OF KNOWING AND DIFFERENT FORMS OF EVIDENCE

The social theorist, Habermas, argues that human communities interpret and share values, stories and cultural norms. These are important elements of human relationships and have their own distinctive ways of knowing. They are best evaluated and described through interpretation and 'softer' means of measurement, such as attitude questionnaires, observation and description. Learning communities build upon and develop these shared values, stories and cultural norms through communication and dialogue.

As well as scientific ways of knowing and interpretive ways of knowing, Habermas argues that human beings and communities are interested in freedom and responsibility, and this finds expression in an emancipatory way of knowing.[2] Here we touch on the moral purpose of schools to 'make a difference' to students, to help them take responsibility for themselves, to overcome those things that hinder, to fulfil their potential and to flourish in society. Emancipatory ways of knowing can only really be evaluated by what the learner, or the individual, says about himself, through self-report and through story. Figure 9.1 shows how different ways of knowing require different forms of evidence, and all of these are important for the moral purpose of schools.

All these forms of knowing are important for learning power, but at the very heart of this relational approach to learning is an 'emancipatory rationality' in which learners are encouraged to take responsibility for their own learning in life. It is also at the heart of school self-evaluation – in which the school takes responsibility for its own vision, its implementation and improvement, within a broad accountability framework.

THE NEW RELATIONSHIP WITH SCHOOLS

The government's new relationship with schools has data and learning at its heart. Self-evaluation, school improvement partners, government inspections and other accountability measures focus upon collecting and making meaning

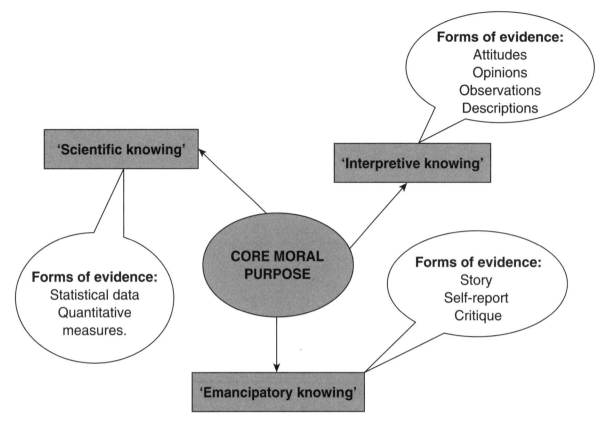

Figure 9.1   Forms of data collection for school self-evaluation

out of complex data, and using this to inform a better future, according to the school's distinctive vision and values.

Schools (and governments) already collect and analyse huge amounts of quantitative data about student attainment – and use this to set targets and direction for future development. Some of that data can identify where students are underachieving and this is perhaps the most 'scientific' element of self-evaluation. The five outcomes of 'Every Child Matters' provide new themes around which schools will need to 'gather evidence'. That is how well schools are helping students to be safe, to be healthy, to enjoy and achieve, to make a positive contribution and to achieve economic well-being. Clearly this will require all three types of data and all three ways of knowing.

The following examples come from the questions posed in a school self-evaluation document, which reflects the school development plan and forms a dynamic basis for reporting to parents and other stakeholders. They are taken from a secondary school, whose head teacher, Ellen, is deeply committed to the school becoming a learner-centred community. They focus on how student self-assessment of learning power, and the assessment of teachers' learner-centred practices, can provide powerful evidence for this process. The examples are not intended to be exhaustive.

How do you gather the views of learners, parents, carers and other stakeholders? How often do you do this and how do you ensure impartiality?

- *Our students complete a learning power profile at the beginning of each academic year. Their profiles tell them, and their teacher, what they think of themselves as learners. They view their own profiles as part of their own self-assessment process and, supported by their tutors, they take responsibility for setting their own 'learning to learn' targets. They evaluate their progress at the end of each unit of work and, with project work, identify which particular learning dimensions are necessary for success.*

- *In addition to this, the students' learning profiles are averaged for each class group, year group and the school as a whole. From this we can identify key areas that need attention. For example, we currently know that students report themselves to be significantly weaker in strategic awareness in Key Stage 3 while, at Key Stage 4, creativity is in need of development. Leading teachers responsible for curriculum and learning ensure that these are addressed at management level.*

- *Students' learning profiles are calculated as percentages and included in the school's assessment information systems. Where students' 'value added' scores suggest that they are underachieving, then learning profiles are interrogated for both explanations and potential strategies.*

- *These data are valid because they come from students themselves. Where a student disagrees with his profile results, then this is moderated and forms the basis of a learning conversation.*

- *The most regular place for conversations and strategy building about learning power for all students is in the tutor group, which meets three times a week. Tutors are responsible for the whole learner – both academic and personal development. Once a term the timetable is suspended and parents are invited in to meet with tutors and learners for a conversation, for which the students' diagrams from their learning profiles and the students' learning journals are a focus.*

- *Teachers are invited to undertake the Assessment of Learner-centred Practices Surveys with a particular class. These surveys provide teachers with systematic evidence of how their students perceive them to be providing a learner-centred environment against the four factors shown by research to significantly improve motivation and achievement:*

  - *Creating positive interpersonal relationships*
  - *Honouring student voice*
  - *Stimulating higher order thinking*
  - *Catering for individual developmental differences.*

- *The gaps between the students' perceptions of their teacher and the teacher's perceptions of himself provide the focus for professional and practical development.*

- *We gather evidence about the 'emotional climate' of our school as a living system through the School's Emotional Environment for Learning Survey,[3] which provides us with data about perceived quality of relationships, how safe students feel in their learning environments, and how well the school is supporting them in feeling valued.*

- *In addition to this we invite a learning research partner to undertake 'focus groups' with students each year. The purpose of these is to gather more data on students' perceptions about the school as a whole and how well it is supporting their learning.*

- *Summaries of all of this information are available to parents and they are invited to comment.*

- *Each head of year tracks two students over the year, and collects from them written and narrative evidence of their particular learning journeys. These are used as exemplars, for action research evidence and further professional learning.*

Table 9.1	Applying the seven learning power dimensions to a school as a living and learning system
Changing and Learning	The school has a culture of professional learning. Leaders are open to new forms of evidence and know how to distil key ideas from current research. The school has a strong sense of its own identity and values. Teachers, governors, parents and students will use these 'values' as a third voice in learning conversations. It is assumed that all 'innovations' will be evaluated in the light of them. Ongoing mini-research projects are the norm for teachers. A significant minority of staff have returned to formal, accredited learning.
Meaning Making	Teachers, particularly the head, are constantly on the look out to make meaning from research, policy and best practice and to 'customise' local and national initiatives to the unique culture of the school. Data gathered routinely is frequently discussed in the staff-room, and teachers are often making connections between 'new' ideas and their experience in the classroom.
Critical Curiosity	Data collected is not taken at face value. There is a 'buzz' around getting to the bottom of a problem – whether that is what to do about a disaffected learner or what sort of assessment management system best supports learning. There is a transparency about 'problems' – they are seen as challenges. There is a long-term commitment to finding solutions rather than a short-term 'quick fix' mentality.
Creativity	Teams of teachers develop their own unique approaches to the curriculum. Teachers are encouraged to do 'blue sky' thinking to solve problems. The school has its own distinctive identity and vision – which is expressed in a unique way. Several teachers regularly go 'on retreats' in which they are encouraged to attend to their 'inner lives' as part of their professional development.
Learning Relationships	Relationships are generally positive. Listening is valued. Trust is high, while individual 'idiosyncrasies' are usually valued and included. Conflict and difference between teachers, or teams, is acknowledged, accepted and discussed as part of life. There is a strong culture of peer evaluation. Teachers are valued and feel valued. There is a high level of organisational emotional literacy. Team work, both in the classroom and in wider school initiatives, is the norm. All members of the community feel they can participate.

Table 9.1	(Continued)
Strategic Awareness	The head teacher leads a team committed to gathering as much information about the organisation as possible. The school development plan is a 'living document' participated in by governors and all leading teachers. Feedback loops are in place at all levels and reflection and evaluation is the norm. The school invites 'critical friend' analysis from colleagues in other schools, in the research community and among policy-makers.
Resilience	The head teacher and her team know that change is incremental and takes time. They don't wait until all the t's have been crossed and the i's dotted before initiating. Set backs are inevitable and change is 'paced' accordingly. When an initiative does not work well it is not abandoned, it is evaluated and adapted. Times of confusion and 'messiness' are considered to be part of changing and learning. The head knows that the key to effective change is people, who carry the school's vision. She invests in people.

PROFESSIONAL LEARNING – A KEY TO A HEALTHY LIVING SYSTEM

It is clear from this example how the self-assessment of learning power can provide rich data of all types for school self-evaluation – where the moral purpose of the school is to promote effective lifelong learners and active citizens. If these forms of evaluation and assessment are conducted regularly and managed electronically, then the school can build up a powerful and ongoing databank of information for organisational learning and reporting purposes.

So far in this book we have explored how learning power can be identified and developed for individual learners and for class groups, and how teachers can become facilitators of learning. This is about self-evaluation for learners and for teachers.

However, we can also apply the seven dimensions of learning power to the school as a living organisation, in order to evaluate the school's organisational learning power.

Table 9.1 takes the seven dimensions of learning power and applies them to a school as a healthy living and learning system, capable of self-evaluation and organisational growth.

So the seven dimensions of learning power can be applied to the school as a living, learning system. Such a community will value its people as learners, and will be enterprising and distinctive in its practice.

Summary

In this chapter we have seen how gathering and using data to inform better practice is at the heart of self-evaluation.

- Learning power is the fuel for school self-evaluation and this can be explored at the level of the individual learner, the teacher and the school as a whole.
- A learning journey requires a destination and a compass. Using the values of learning power to fuel self-evaluation enables schools to measure progress against their own goals as well as providing impressive evidence for public accountability.
- Evidence can be 'scientific', 'interpretive' or 'emancipatory'. A healthy learning community will gather different types of evidence for different purposes.

 ## NOTES AND FURTHER READING

1. See this famous, anonymous, letter written by a Holocaust survivor:

    Dear Teacher,

    I am a survivor of a concentration camp. My eyes saw what no man should witness: Gas chambers built by learned engineers. Children poisoned by educated physicians. Infants killed by trained nurses. Women and babies shot and burned by high school and college graduates. So, I am suspicious of education.

    My request is: Help your students become human. Your efforts must never produce learned monsters, skilled psychopaths, educated Eichmanns. Reading, writing, arithmetic are important only if they serve to make our children more human.

    From *Facing History and Ourselves: Holocaust and Human Behaviour*, a resource book available from: http://www.facinghistory.org/.

2. Sergiovanni, T. (2000) *The Lifeworld of Leadership Creating Culture, Community and Personal Meaning in Our Schools*. San Francisco, CA: Jossey Bass.
3. School Emotional Environment for Learning Survey (SEELS) – an online self-evaluation tool available from: www.antidote.org.uk.

Chapter 10

Learning power and education for citizenship and enterprise

In this final chapter we shall explore the relationship between learning power and education for citizenship and enterprise. We shall see how a learner-centred classroom and school provide a fertile ecology for:

- skills for enterprise
- aptitudes and dispositions for citizenship
- community-based learning.

Citizenship education is about preparing young people for active participation in democratic societies. Across the world there is agreement among policy-makers and teachers to incorporate this in school curricula. Although the ideas are as old as education itself, it has a new 'spin' in our contemporary, global society, with its risks, challenges and threats. More than ever we need independent-minded, critical and socially aware 'citizens' who are able to honour their own traditions and values and yet adapt and contribute to the changing world in which we live.

Different countries use different terminology and have different emphases, but the three strands of citizenship education which provide a framework for English schools[1] are a useful way of understanding the challenge to educators. These are:

- Moral and social development
- Political literacy
- Community involvement.

While there is a body of knowledge about democratic processes that students need to know, this is not in itself sufficient for effective citizenship education. Students' moral and social development and their capacity to critically engage with their communities – in a manner that both enhances their learning and makes a contribution – are part of the picture to be addressed by all teachers and school leaders. It crosses the usual boundaries between subjects and between 'in school' and 'out of school' learning.

Schools that have a learner-centred culture, in which students' learning power is strengthened through integrating academic and personal development, are schools well placed to be effective in citizenship education.

TOURO COLLEGE LIBRARY

CHARACTERISTICS OF 'CITIZENSHIP' SCHOOLS

Research shows that where teachers and schools take citizenship education seriously, significant lessons emerge from the way they do things.[2] The whole school is implicated – everything that goes on contributes to, or detracts from, citizenship education. In a nutshell, such schools are learner centred, focusing on the learner and the process of learning itself. They will stimulate higher order thinking skills, and will have classrooms characterised by dialogue in which there is a high level of participation by students, both in their own learning processes and in the ways their classrooms and schools are managed. Teachers will be facilitators of learning, and that learning will be relevant to the narratives of the students' own lives and experiences. In short, such schools are developing responsible learners who know how to engage actively with the world in which they live. Figure 10.1 summarises the evidence from research about how citizenship education influences what schools do.

PARTICIPATION

Active participation by students in learning, and in how the school runs, is a model of democratic activity, and embodies the fundamental human right of self-determination. Such participation, and the responsibilities that arise out of it, are integral to citizenship education *and* to the development of learning power. They are incompatible with highly controlling teaching styles and authoritarian rules; they require instead a high degree of structured support for students to take responsibility for their own learning and personal development. This means teachers 'letting go' of control aimed simply at compliance, which risks closing down options, reducing motivation and disenfranchising learners, and concentrating instead on developing responsibility in students and sharing it with them. These sorts of practices, and the planning and actions needed to stimulate and manage participative dialogue and discourse in the classroom, can only happen in a climate of trust where teachers and their professional judgements are supported by leaders and administrators. Participation is an indispensable part of the ecology of learning power.

THE CURRICULUM: SCAFFOLDING OR CAGE?

A learner-friendly and citizenship-oriented school has a flexible, and imaginative approach to the curriculum, however tightly prescribed it may be by government and by external assessments. It will view the curriculum framework as scaffolding or a platform rather than a cage. The way the curriculum is structured, together with the way progress and outcomes are assessed, will either enhance or inhibit a learner-centred culture. A balance is needed between the content requirements of the curriculum, the concepts and skills students need to acquire in a rigorous and planned way and the processes involved in developing learners who are able and willing to take responsibility for their own learning power.

LEARNING AND TEACHING

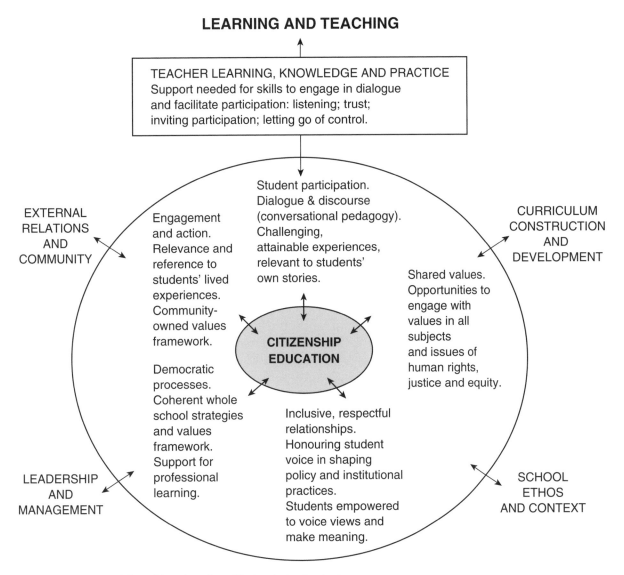

TEACHER LEARNING, KNOWLEDGE AND PRACTICE
Support needed for skills to engage in dialogue
and facilitate participation: listening; trust;
inviting participation; letting go of control.

EXTERNAL
RELATIONS
AND
COMMUNITY

Engagement
and action.
Relevance and
reference to
students' lived
experiences.
Community-
owned values
framework.

Student participation.
Dialogue & discourse
(conversational pedagogy).
Challenging,
attainable experiences,
relevant to students'
own stories.

CURRICULUM
CONSTRUCTION
AND
DEVELOPMENT

Shared values.
Opportunities to
engage with
values in all
subjects
and issues of
human rights,
justice and equity.

**CITIZENSHIP
EDUCATION**

Democratic
processes.
Coherent whole
school strategies
and values
framework.
Support for
professional
learning.

Inclusive, respectful
relationships.
Honouring student
voice in shaping
policy and institutional
practices.
Students empowered
to voice views and
make meaning.

LEADERSHIP
AND
MANAGEMENT

SCHOOL
ETHOS
AND CONTEXT

Figure 10.1   How citizenship education affects what schools do

'BOTTOM UP' EXCAVATION FOR MEANING

There is a particular tension here for secondary schools which, as we have seen, tend to have a more subject-dominated curriculum structure and an increasing focus on external assessments. When knowledge is encountered from the starting point of a real problem, which the student recognises and is motivated to explore for answers, then the student is naturally invited to deploy the different dimensions of learning power and will inevitably encounter questions of social values embedded in all human experience.

This is a 'bottom up' approach to knowledge, rather than a 'top down' one. In the latter, the ideas and concepts are presented first in the abstract and then only later, if at all, applied to the real-life experience of the learner. In the former the student has to do her own digging for information and constructs her own meaning from the evidence she gathers. In the process she will be 'flexing her own learning muscles' as well as forming her own values and opinions.

Where the student chooses her own starting point for a problem-based enquiry, then motivation and personal meaning will be strong.

Mapping values onto schemes of work

Look at a unit of work in your subject area. Can you identify places where there are natural encounters with your school's core values?

They may be implicit in the content, the application or the process.

Try foregrounding an encounter with these values as a learning objective in science, or maths. Make use of story as a 'way in'.

The values of justice, truthfulness and sustainability are particularly relevant to citizenship – and these values are naturally embedded in most schemes of work across the subjects. They are core values, which many learning communities have as ideals and recognise as part of the traditions and history of their communities. Young people also recognise these values in operation in their own lives and stories – even if they are not able to articulate them. Very young children have a strong sense of justice or fairness, and recognise truthfulness when they see it. They readily understand 'caring for each other' and the need to 'take care of' people and things.

While these values are ones which are likely to be embraced by most learning communities, the ways in which they are expressed and the particular combination of values and the language will vary each time, as will the degree of 'authenticity' – that is, how much the community LIVES the values as well as TALKING about them. On the one hand a set of values can be dismissed as 'motherhood and apple pie' – something that everyone thinks is a good thing but so what? On the other hand they could be dismissed as 'authoritarian' and a source of 'imposed' morality, which is not at all educative. Neither is the case. In a dynamic, learner-centred culture, it does not matter that we may not agree on the exact meaning of our community's core values – what is important is that they form a 'third voice' in learning dialogues. In fact, learning power is essential for a critical dialogue with our own and our society's values and the values of 'different' groups within our communities. These differing sets of values and stories need to be continually challenged as well as 'owned'. Schools can (and should) be places where critical challenge is 'encouraged' and 'difference' celebrated. This is their educative function.

LEARNING AT THE INTERSECTION OF THREE STORIES

Meaningful learning takes place when three stories connect: the personal stories; stories of the community and society; and the stories implicit in the subject matter of what is being learned (see Figure 10.2). Most of us understand ourselves, our communities and our world through the telling of stories. Just ask anyone what is really important to them and they are likely to tell you a story. How we tell and re-tell our stories is a key element of personal growth and development.

The dimensions of learning power enable us to make these connections between the different stories. Values, such as sustainability or justice, are accessed and understood through those stories. Asking the question 'what is the story behind this?' is a powerful way of making meaning, and of developing dialogue and critical thinking. It is also getting at questions of values and critical thinking.

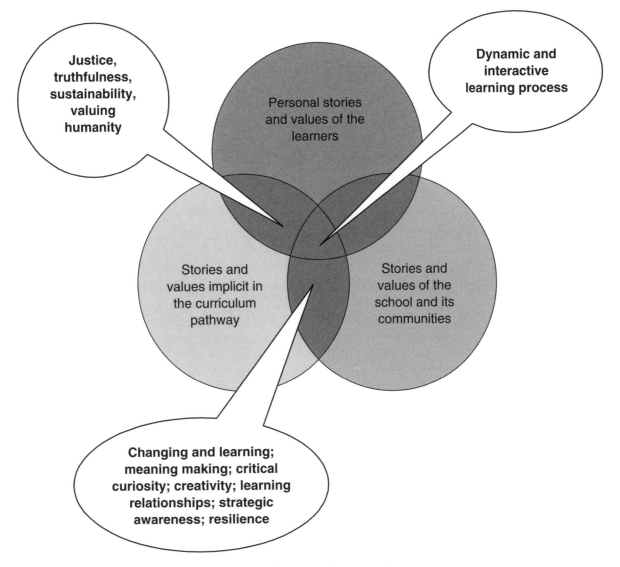

Figure 10.2 Developing responsible learners: a three-storied conversation

This approach to learning is at the heart of effective citizenship education. It does not replace a rigorous and planned approach to students' acquisition of the knowledge, skills and understanding necessary for active democratic engagement, but is a necessary foundation for the dispositions, values and attitudes which underpin a civil society.

CHARACTERISTICS OF TEACHING FOR CITIZENSHIP EDUCATION

The messages from research have been captured in a list of helpful and unhelpful tactics for teachers wanting to foster citizenship education in their classrooms, set out below.[3] The list could equally apply to the development of learning power.

Teachers wanting to promote citizenship education might wish to consider doing more of this:

Dialogue

- listen to students, as individuals as well as groups
- encourage them to pose questions of their own rather than simply answer those posed for them
- coach them in asking 'why?' and 'how?' questions and refusing to accept propositions at face value
- admit to 'not knowing' but suggest how to find out
- take time out to get to know individuals in their own right
  - create opportunities for sharing personal 'stories and journeys' and relating programmes of work to them
  - make judgements about the degree of responsibility that can confidently be expected of each individual at every stage

Participation

- ensure that all students are included and involved in ways that suit their learning needs
- model and encourage relationships characterised by trust, affirmation and challenge
- progressively and safely 'let go' of the need or desire to control things single-handedly and make explicit everyone's personal and collective responsibility for respectful, orderly conduct and collaboration
- involve students in formulating the expectations and 'ground rules' which create the conditions for respectful dialogue and discourse
- take responsibility for upholding these and periodically renewing commitment to them
- confront and clarify any apparently deliberate attempt to undermine or subvert such agreed 'ground rules' and take appropriate and predictable action
- organise and (with the students' help) continually re-organise the classroom so as to indicate the equal value of every voice and facilitate face-to-face dialogue between pairs, in groups and in the whole-class forum

Empowering learners – empowering teachers

- build in time for reflection, for themselves and their students
- reflect back to individuals and groups the learning about citizenship that they are achieving through collaborative processes as well as content and output
- include these intended learning outcomes in the objectives they plan for and make them explicit at the start of sessions
- involve learners in structured self-evaluation and inform their own assessment judgements by this means
- inform themselves about the rights and responsibilities of citizenship, including matters of justice, ethics, equity and equality, lawful and unlawful discrimination, social formation, economic awareness, democratic

accountability and participation, public and private finance and account-ability, political pressures and processes of government, civic and human rights

- allow students to practise articulating their own social vision and values while encouraging a critical, questioning response
- coach students in the same skills
- encourage learners to develop criteria for the validation of opinions, atti-tudes and beliefs
- practise reflective self-evaluation, with the help of professional 'critical friends' and monitor the extent to which their teaching models and expresses (non-verbally as well as verbally) the values of citizenship education;

... and less of this:

- ask more questions than their students
- say more than all the class put together
- ask questions to which they already know the answers
- see themselves as the main repository of knowledge or wisdom
- use the content and knowledge-base of the curriculum as the sole organ-ising principle for their planning
- arrange students permanently in rows of desks facing the front
- use their power to suggest an unequal right to opinions, attitudes and beliefs
- suggest that there are simple, right and wrong answers or 'quick fix' solu-tions to matters of personal and social morality
- assume that learners understand why they are there and what they are intended to learn
- keep criteria for assessment judgements to themselves and impose those judgements summarily and without explanation.

EDUCATION FOR ENTERPRISE

Enterprise education is about helping young people to make things happen, to be creative and to find opportunities for themselves.[4] Problem solving and team work, creativity, resilience, emotional intelligence, evaluative skills and responsible decision making are regularly identified as necessary personal qualities for people who are going to be enterprising in their personal and professional lives.

Enterprise capabilities

The ability to handle uncertainty and respond positively to change, to create and implement new ideas and ways of doing things, to make reasonable risk/reward assessments and act on them in one's personal and working life...

(Davies, 2002)

Creativity is particularly sought after around the world, since constant change at all levels is characteristic of life in the twenty-first century. Creativity depends on the ability to bring together ideas and insights from different fields in order to create new ways of doing and thinking. It requires giving free rein to intuition and imagination and allowing new com-binations of ideas to emerge in different ways. Taking risks, or moving into the 'unknown', is a characteristic of creativity and requires trust in oneself and in the learning community. It is relevant across the disciplines.

ENTERPRISE AND LEARNING POWER ARE 'SOUL SISTERS'

The skills necessary for enterprise (Davies, 2002) are 'soul sisters' of the dimensions of learning power. Where you find one, the other will not be far away.

An enterprising curriculum is a learner-centred one, in which learners are encouraged to choose their own learning pathways and become aware of and develop their own learning power.

Typically, schools pioneering new approaches to education for enterprise adopt a 'project based' or 'modular' approach to part of the curriculum, where interdisciplinary enquiry is necessary and students are invited to identify and solve problems. The learning can be based around a set of competencies (as with the Opening Minds Curriculum[5]) or around a problem to be solved. Students begin with a focus on something in 'the real world' which forms a starting point for their 'excavations'. They manage and evaluate their own learning pathways, presenting the outcomes of their learning and a commentary on the skills, aptitudes and dispositions they have developed as part of the final product.

WHERE IS THE LEARNING IN SERVICE LEARNING?

Community involvement is a feature of citizenship education – sometimes this is called 'service learning'. All too often however, it is little more than charitable work and it is hard to see any citizenship education taking place. By integrating a 'bottom up', competency-based curriculum with community involvement and with enterprise, it becomes easy to see how the development of learning power and learning for citizenship and enterprise can be developed as part of a planned, monitored and assessed curriculum.

The example of a unit of work set out in Figure 10.3 is an integrated 'bottom up' project which leads learners into active involvement in the community, addressing issues of citizenship and enterprise as part of their 'mainstream' learning.

AN INTEGRATED APPROACH

The dispositions, values and attitudes necessary for effective lifelong learning are very close to those necessary for the development of enterprising adults and active and positively contributing citizens. Rather than seeing all of these initiatives as extra, add-on demands to an already overfilled curriculum, schools can integrate them through creative leadership and thus provide a more holistic experience for students. Perhaps the key idea in all of these themes has to do with changing and learning – in response to the complex social and economic realities of life in the twenty-first century: Changing and

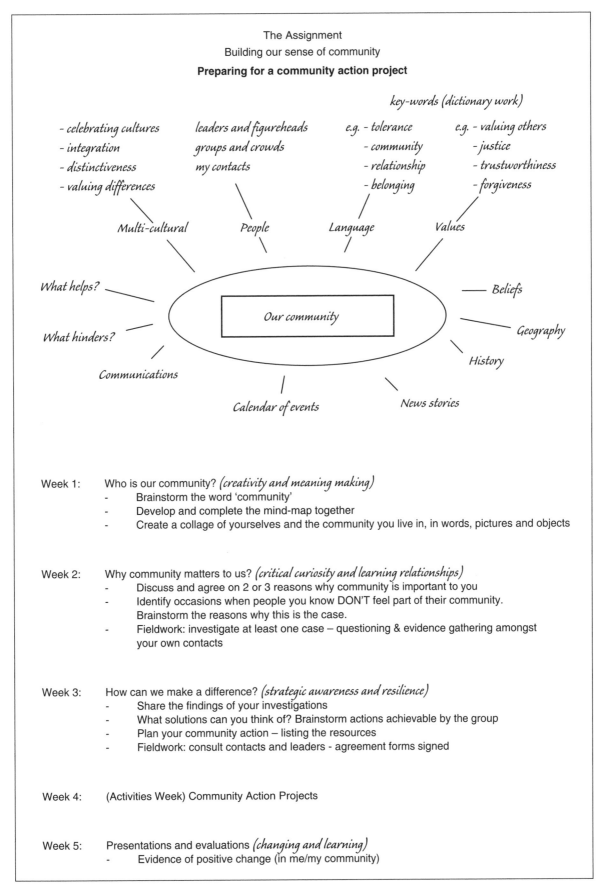

The Assignment
Building our sense of community
Preparing for a community action project

key-words (dictionary work)

- *celebrating cultures*
- *integration*
- *distinctiveness*
- *valuing differences*

leaders and figureheads
groups and crowds
my contacts

e.g. - tolerance
- community
- relationship
- belonging

e.g. - valuing others
- justice
- trustworthiness
- forgiveness

Multi-cultural   *People*   *Language*   *Values*

What helps?

What hinders?

Our community

Beliefs

Geography

History

Communications

Calendar of events

News stories

Week 1:   Who is our community? *(creativity and meaning making)*
-   Brainstorm the word 'community'
-   Develop and complete the mind-map together
-   Create a collage of yourselves and the community you live in, in words, pictures and objects

Week 2:   Why community matters to us? *(critical curiosity and learning relationships)*
-   Discuss and agree on 2 or 3 reasons why community is important to you
-   Identify occasions when people you know DON'T feel part of their community. Brainstorm the reasons why this is the case.
-   Fieldwork: investigate at least one case – questioning & evidence gathering amongst your own contacts

Week 3:   How can we make a difference? *(strategic awareness and resilience)*
-   Share the findings of your investigations
-   What solutions can you think of? Brainstorm actions achievable by the group
-   Plan your community action – listing the resources
-   Fieldwork: consult contacts and leaders - agreement forms signed

Week 4:   (Activities Week) Community Action Projects

Week 5:   Presentations and evaluations *(changing and learning)*
-   Evidence of positive change (in me/my community)

Figure 10.3   The Assignment: Building our sense of community

learning that are at the same time deeply personal as well as public. Nothing could be more relevant to the challenges, threats and opportunities of our global community.

Summary

In this final chapter we have explored the links between learning power and education for citizenship and enterprise. We have seen how learner centredness provides a basis for both citizenship and enterprise. In particular we have seen that:

- the dispositions, values and attitudes necessary for learning power are also important for citizenship and enterprise
- a 'bottom up' approach to the content of the curriculum requires students to encounter social values relevant for citizenship
- changing and learning are the essential components of a dynamic response to the complex demands of life in a changing and challenging world.

 # NOTES AND FURTHER READING

1. Crick, B. (1998) *Education for Citizenship and the Teaching of Democracy in Schools: Final Report of the Advisory Group on Citizenship*. London: Qualifications and Curriculum Authority.

2. For systematic reviews of evidence from around the world about citizenship education, see:

   Deakin Crick, R., Coates, M., Taylor, M. and Ritchie, S. (2004) 'A systematic review of the impact of citizenship education on the provision of schooling', in *Research Evidence in Education Library*. London: Evidence for Policy and Practice Information and Co-ordinating Centre, Social Science Research Unit, Institute of Education.
   Deakin Crick, R., Tew, M., Taylor, M. Durant, K. and Samuel, E. (2005) 'A systematic review of the impact of citizenship education on learning and achievement', in *Research Evidence in Education Library*. London: Evidence for Policy and Practice Information and Co-ordinating Centre, Social Science Research Unit, Institute of Education.

3. The findings of the first review are summarised in the following booklet: Small, T. (2004) *Developing Citizenship in Schools: Implications for Teachers and Students Arising from the EPPI Review of the Impact of Citizenship Education on the Provision of Schooling*. Bristol: Citizenship Education Review Group.

4. Davies, H. (2002) *A Review of Enterprise and Economy in Education*. London: Department for Education and Skills.

5. RSA (2005) *Opening Minds: Giving Young People a Better Chance*. London: Royal Society for the encouragement of Arts, Manufactures & Commerce.

The Rhythm Of Learning Song

The mystery of learning
Was still to behold
Many have tried to uncover
Now the story will be told

We are the learning creatures
We live at Westbury Park
We are the learning creatures
When the fun begins let's start

My name is Vinny the vulture
High in the sky I'm king
I see the world like a jigsaw
Meaning making is my thing

I'm Gerard the giraffe
I like asking questions
Questions help us find answers
Answers help us all to learn

I'm Marvin them monkey
I swing to new ideas
I like to be original
So let's all give me three cheers

My name is Carmen Crocodile
I'm strategically aware
I've got a toolkit of strategies
Solving problems everywhere

I'm Elli the elephant
I enjoy making friends
Learning is great together
Arguments I can mend

I'm Lenny Lion
Resilience is my thing
When we say 'We can not do it!'
Lenny just jumps right in

I'm Camilla Chameleon
I know my brain can expand
Learning can only get better
Join my learning rhythm band

by Class 5M, Westbury Park School

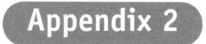

Appendix 2

The Learning Power Flashcards

The Learning power Flashcards, available here for you to photocopy and cut out, are designed for learners (and their teachers!) to use for themselves. Once you have started working with Learning Power ideas, just choose an ELLI dimension that you want to concentrate on. Keep the flashcard with you and check it out from time to time when you are learning, at home or at school. It will help you to improve your learning power by yourself as well as in class. When you are ready, choose another one. Aim to become an all-round, highly effective lifelong learner!

© Ruth Deakin Crick and Tim Small, *Learning Power in Practice*, Paul Chapman Publishing, 2006

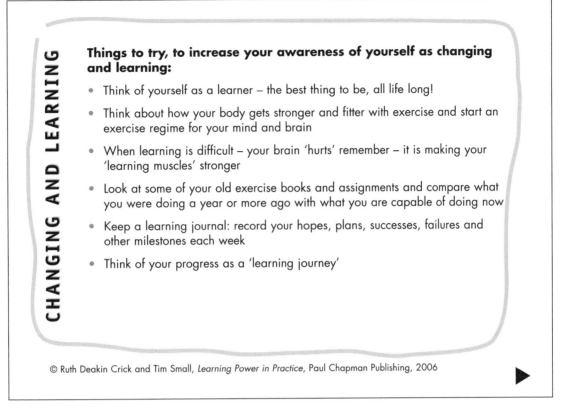

CHANGING AND LEARNING

Things to try, to increase your awareness of yourself as changing and learning:

- Think of yourself as a learner – the best thing to be, all life long!

- Think about how your body gets stronger and fitter with exercise and start an exercise regime for your mind and brain

- When learning is difficult – your brain 'hurts' remember – it is making your 'learning muscles' stronger

- Look at some of your old exercise books and assignments and compare what you were doing a year or more ago with what you are capable of doing now

- Keep a learning journal: record your hopes, plans, successes, failures and other milestones each week

- Think of your progress as a 'learning journey'

© Ruth Deakin Crick and Tim Small, *Learning Power in Practice*, Paul Chapman Publishing, 2006

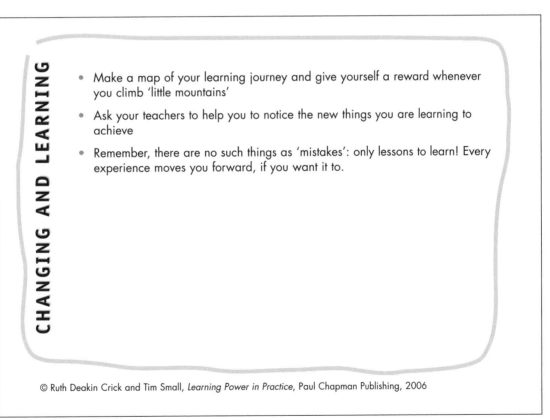

CHANGING AND LEARNING

- Make a map of your learning journey and give yourself a reward whenever you climb 'little mountains'

- Ask your teachers to help you to notice the new things you are learning to achieve

- Remember, there are no such things as 'mistakes': only lessons to learn! Every experience moves you forward, if you want it to.

© Ruth Deakin Crick and Tim Small, *Learning Power in Practice*, Paul Chapman Publishing, 2006

P **This page can be photocopied and cut out**

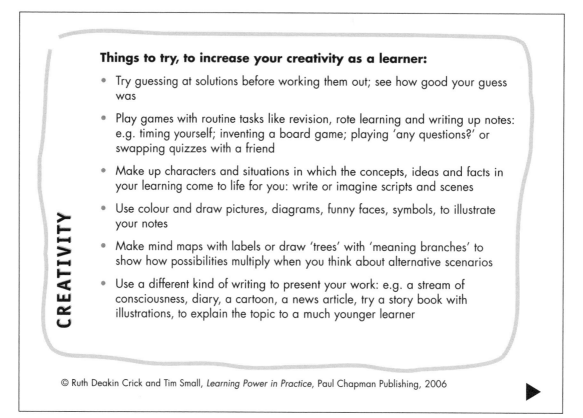

Things to try, to increase your creativity as a learner:

- Try guessing at solutions before working them out; see how good your guess was

- Play games with routine tasks like revision, rote learning and writing up notes: e.g. timing yourself; inventing a board game; playing 'any questions?' or swapping quizzes with a friend

- Make up characters and situations in which the concepts, ideas and facts in your learning come to life for you: write or imagine scripts and scenes

- Use colour and draw pictures, diagrams, funny faces, symbols, to illustrate your notes

- Make mind maps with labels or draw 'trees' with 'meaning branches' to show how possibilities multiply when you think about alternative scenarios

- Use a different kind of writing to present your work: e.g. a stream of consciousness, diary, a cartoon, a news article, try a story book with illustrations, to explain the topic to a much younger learner

CREATIVITY

© Ruth Deakin Crick and Tim Small, *Learning Power in Practice*, Paul Chapman Publishing, 2006

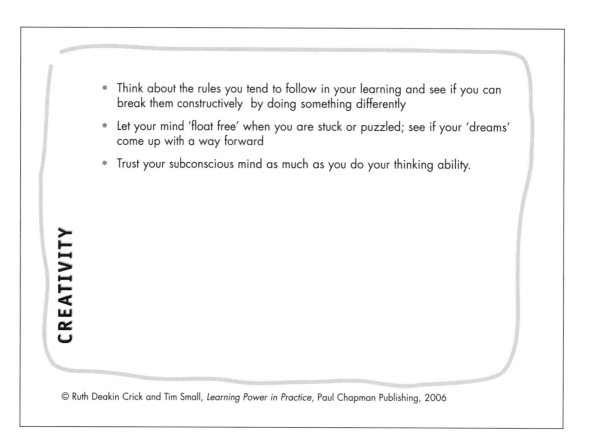

- Think about the rules you tend to follow in your learning and see if you can break them constructively by doing something differently

- Let your mind 'float free' when you are stuck or puzzled; see if your 'dreams' come up with a way forward

- Trust your subconscious mind as much as you do your thinking ability.

CREATIVITY

© Ruth Deakin Crick and Tim Small, *Learning Power in Practice*, Paul Chapman Publishing, 2006

P   **This page can be photocopied and cut out**

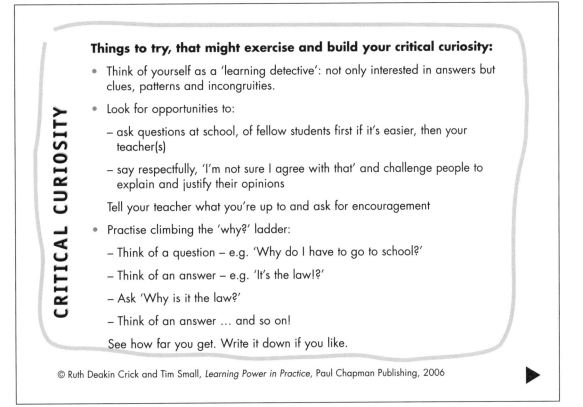

CRITICAL CURIOSITY

Things to try, that might exercise and build your critical curiosity:

- Think of yourself as a 'learning detective': not only interested in answers but clues, patterns and incongruities.

- Look for opportunities to:

  – ask questions at school, of fellow students first if it's easier, then your teacher(s)

  – say respectfully, 'I'm not sure I agree with that' and challenge people to explain and justify their opinions

  Tell your teacher what you're up to and ask for encouragement

- Practise climbing the 'why?' ladder:

  – Think of a question – e.g. 'Why do I have to go to school?'

  – Think of an answer – e.g. 'It's the law!?'

  – Ask 'Why is it the law?'

  – Think of an answer ... and so on!

  See how far you get. Write it down if you like.

© Ruth Deakin Crick and Tim Small, *Learning Power in Practice*, Paul Chapman Publishing, 2006

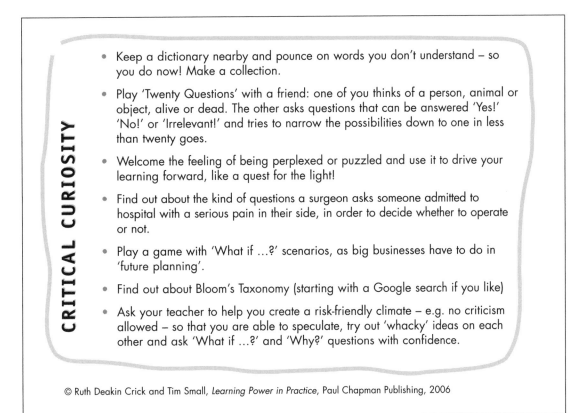

CRITICAL CURIOSITY

- Keep a dictionary nearby and pounce on words you don't understand – so you do now! Make a collection.

- Play 'Twenty Questions' with a friend: one of you thinks of a person, animal or object, alive or dead. The other asks questions that can be answered 'Yes!' 'No!' or 'Irrelevant!' and tries to narrow the possibilities down to one in less than twenty goes.

- Welcome the feeling of being perplexed or puzzled and use it to drive your learning forward, like a quest for the light!

- Find out about the kind of questions a surgeon asks someone admitted to hospital with a serious pain in their side, in order to decide whether to operate or not.

- Play a game with 'What if ...?' scenarios, as big businesses have to do in 'future planning'.

- Find out about Bloom's Taxonomy (starting with a Google search if you like)

- Ask your teacher to help you create a risk-friendly climate – e.g. no criticism allowed – so that you are able to speculate, try out 'whacky' ideas on each other and ask 'What if ...?' and 'Why?' questions with confidence.

© Ruth Deakin Crick and Tim Small, *Learning Power in Practice*, Paul Chapman Publishing, 2006

P **This page can be photocopied and cut out**

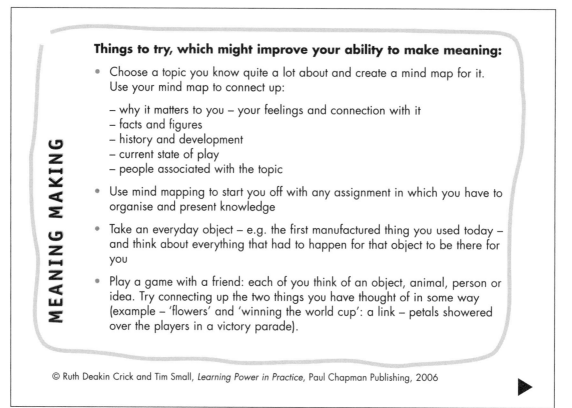

MEANING MAKING

Things to try, which might improve your ability to make meaning:

- Choose a topic you know quite a lot about and create a mind map for it. Use your mind map to connect up:

  – why it matters to you – your feelings and connection with it
  – facts and figures
  – history and development
  – current state of play
  – people associated with the topic

- Use mind mapping to start you off with any assignment in which you have to organise and present knowledge

- Take an everyday object – e.g. the first manufactured thing you used today – and think about everything that had to happen for that object to be there for you

- Play a game with a friend: each of you think of an object, animal, person or idea. Try connecting up the two things you have thought of in some way (example – 'flowers' and 'winning the world cup': a link – petals showered over the players in a victory parade).

© Ruth Deakin Crick and Tim Small, *Learning Power in Practice*, Paul Chapman Publishing, 2006

▶

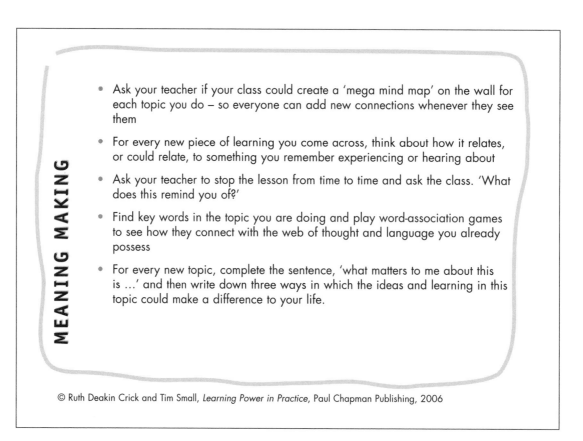

MEANING MAKING

- Ask your teacher if your class could create a 'mega mind map' on the wall for each topic you do – so everyone can add new connections whenever they see them

- For every new piece of learning you come across, think about how it relates, or could relate, to something you remember experiencing or hearing about

- Ask your teacher to stop the lesson from time to time and ask the class. 'What does this remind you of?'

- Find key words in the topic you are doing and play word-association games to see how they connect with the web of thought and language you already possess

- For every new topic, complete the sentence, 'what matters to me about this is ...' and then write down three ways in which the ideas and learning in this topic could make a difference to your life.

© Ruth Deakin Crick and Tim Small, *Learning Power in Practice*, Paul Chapman Publishing, 2006

P **This page can be photocopied and cut out**

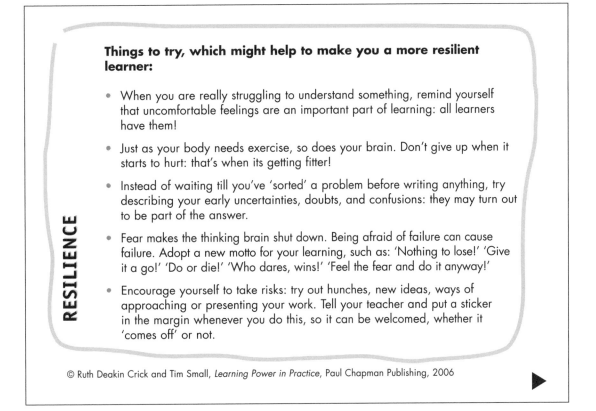

Things to try, which might help to make you a more resilient learner:

- When you are really struggling to understand something, remind yourself that uncomfortable feelings are an important part of learning: all learners have them!

- Just as your body needs exercise, so does your brain. Don't give up when it starts to hurt: that's when its getting fitter!

- Instead of waiting till you've 'sorted' a problem before writing anything, try describing your early uncertainties, doubts, and confusions: they may turn out to be part of the answer.

- Fear makes the thinking brain shut down. Being afraid of failure can cause failure. Adopt a new motto for your learning, such as: 'Nothing to lose!' 'Give it a go!' 'Do or die!' 'Who dares, wins!' 'Feel the fear and do it anyway!'

- Encourage yourself to take risks: try out hunches, new ideas, ways of approaching or presenting your work. Tell your teacher and put a sticker in the margin whenever you do this, so it can be welcomed, whether it 'comes off' or not.

RESILIENCE

© Ruth Deakin Crick and Tim Small, *Learning Power in Practice*, Paul Chapman Publishing, 2006

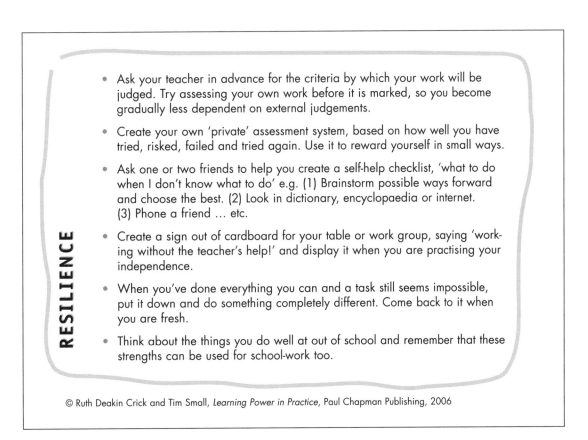

- Ask your teacher in advance for the criteria by which your work will be judged. Try assessing your own work before it is marked, so you become gradually less dependent on external judgements.

- Create your own 'private' assessment system, based on how well you have tried, risked, failed and tried again. Use it to reward yourself in small ways.

- Ask one or two friends to help you create a self-help checklist, 'what to do when I don't know what to do' e.g. (1) Brainstorm possible ways forward and choose the best. (2) Look in dictionary, encyclopaedia or internet. (3) Phone a friend … etc.

- Create a sign out of cardboard for your table or work group, saying 'working without the teacher's help!' and display it when you are practising your independence.

- When you've done everything you can and a task still seems impossible, put it down and do something completely different. Come back to it when you are fresh.

- Think about the things you do well at out of school and remember that these strengths can be used for school-work too.

RESILIENCE

© Ruth Deakin Crick and Tim Small, *Learning Power in Practice*, Paul Chapman Publishing, 2006

P **This page can be photocopied and cut out**

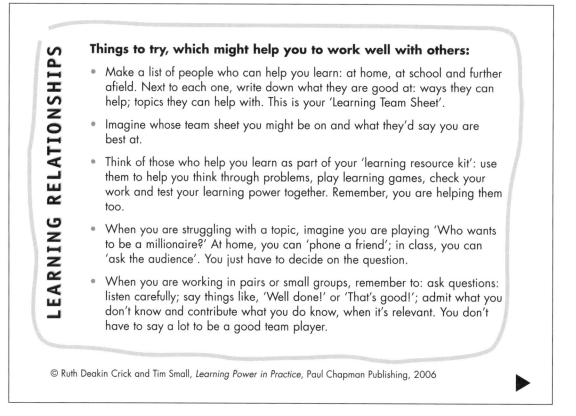

LEARNING RELATIONSHIPS

Things to try, which might help you to work well with others:

- Make a list of people who can help you learn: at home, at school and further afield. Next to each one, write down what they are good at: ways they can help; topics they can help with. This is your 'Learning Team Sheet'.

- Imagine whose team sheet you might be on and what they'd say you are best at.

- Think of those who help you learn as part of your 'learning resource kit': use them to help you think through problems, play learning games, check your work and test your learning power together. Remember, you are helping them too.

- When you are struggling with a topic, imagine you are playing 'Who wants to be a millionaire?' At home, you can 'phone a friend'; in class, you can 'ask the audience'. You just have to decide on the question.

- When you are working in pairs or small groups, remember to: ask questions: listen carefully; say things like, 'Well done!' or 'That's good!'; admit what you don't know and contribute what you do know, when it's relevant. You don't have to say a lot to be a good team player.

© Ruth Deakin Crick and Tim Small, *Learning Power in Practice*, Paul Chapman Publishing, 2006

▶

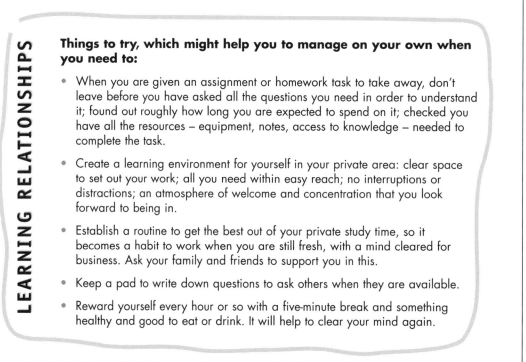

LEARNING RELATIONSHIPS

Things to try, which might help you to manage on your own when you need to:

- When you are given an assignment or homework task to take away, don't leave before you have asked all the questions you need in order to understand it; found out roughly how long you are expected to spend on it; checked you have all the resources – equipment, notes, access to knowledge – needed to complete the task.

- Create a learning environment for yourself in your private area: clear space to set out your work; all you need within easy reach; no interruptions or distractions; an atmosphere of welcome and concentration that you look forward to being in.

- Establish a routine to get the best out of your private study time, so it becomes a habit to work when you are still fresh, with a mind cleared for business. Ask your family and friends to support you in this.

- Keep a pad to write down questions to ask others when they are available.

- Reward yourself every hour or so with a five-minute break and something healthy and good to eat or drink. It will help to clear your mind again.

© Ruth Deakin Crick and Tim Small, *Learning Power in Practice*, Paul Chapman Publishing, 2006

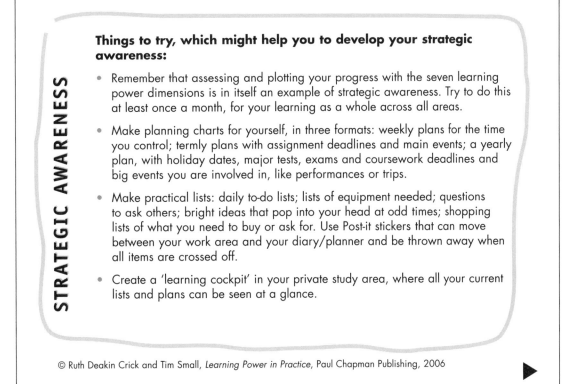

STRATEGIC AWARENESS

Things to try, which might help you to develop your strategic awareness:

- Remember that assessing and plotting your progress with the seven learning power dimensions is in itself an example of strategic awareness. Try to do this at least once a month, for your learning as a whole across all areas.

- Make planning charts for yourself, in three formats: weekly plans for the time you control; termly plans with assignment deadlines and main events; a yearly plan, with holiday dates, major tests, exams and coursework deadlines and big events you are involved in, like performances or trips.

- Make practical lists: daily to-do lists; lists of equipment needed; questions to ask others; bright ideas that pop into your head at odd times; shopping lists of what you need to buy or ask for. Use Post-it stickers that can move between your work area and your diary/planner and be thrown away when all items are crossed off.

- Create a 'learning cockpit' in your private study area, where all your current lists and plans can be seen at a glance.

© Ruth Deakin Crick and Tim Small, *Learning Power in Practice*, Paul Chapman Publishing, 2006

▶

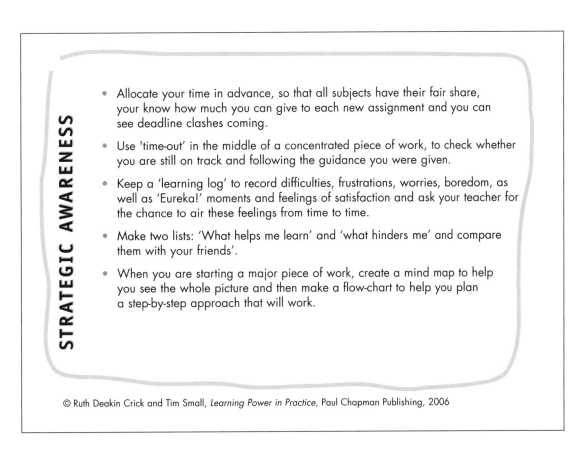

STRATEGIC AWARENESS

- Allocate your time in advance, so that all subjects have their fair share, your know how much you can give to each new assignment and you can see deadline clashes coming.

- Use 'time-out' in the middle of a concentrated piece of work, to check whether you are still on track and following the guidance you were given.

- Keep a 'learning log' to record difficulties, frustrations, worries, boredom, as well as 'Eureka!' moments and feelings of satisfaction and ask your teacher for the chance to air these feelings from time to time.

- Make two lists: 'What helps me learn' and 'what hinders me' and compare them with your friends'.

- When you are starting a major piece of work, create a mind map to help you see the whole picture and then make a flow-chart to help you plan a step-by-step approach that will work.

© Ruth Deakin Crick and Tim Small, *Learning Power in Practice*, Paul Chapman Publishing, 2006

P **This page can be photocopied and cut out**

BIBLIOGRAPHY

Antidote (2004) *The Emotional Literacy Handbook.* London: Antidote. **www.antidote.org.uk** (accessed April 2006).

APA Task Force on Psychology in Education (1993) *Learner-centered Psychological Principles: A Framework for School Redesign and Reform* (Revised Edition). Washington, DC: American Psychological Association and Mid-Continent Regional Educational Laboratory. **www.apa.org** (accessed April 2006).

Assessment Reform Group (1999) *Assessment for Learning: Beyond the Black Box.* Cambridge: University of Cambridge School of Education.

Assessment Reform Group (2002) *Testing, Motivation and Learning.* Cambridge: Assessment Reform Group.

Bond, T. (2004) *Ethical Guidelines for Researching Counselling and Psychotherapy.* Rugby: British Association for Counselling and Psychotherapy.

Clark, E. (1997) *Designing and Implementing an Integrated Curriculum.* Brandon, VT: Holistic Education Press.

Claxton, G. (1997) *Hare Brain, Tortoise Mind: Why Intelligence Increases When You Think Less.* London: Fourth Estate.

Claxton, G. (1999) *Wise Up: The Challenge of Lifelong Learning.* London: Bloomsbury.

Claxton, G. (2002) *Building Learning Power: Helping Young People Become Better Learners.* Bristol: TLO.

Crick, B. (1998) *Education for Citizenship and the Teaching of Democracy in Schools: Final Report of the Advisory Group on Citizenship.* London: Qualifications and Curriculum Authority.

Davies, H. (2002) *A Review of Enterprise and Economy in Education.* London: Department for Education and Skills.

Deakin Crick, R., Broadfoot P. and Claxton, G. (2004) 'Developing an Effective Lifelong Learning Inventory: The Elli Projects', *Assessment for Education*, 11 (3), 247–72.

Deakin Crick, R., Coates, M., Taylor M. and Ritchie, S. (2004) 'A systematic review of the impact of citizenship education on the provision of schooling', in *Research Evidence in Education Library.* London: Evidence for Policy and Practice Information and Co-ordinating Centre, Social Science Research Unit, Institute of Education.

Deakin Crick, R., Tew, M., Taylor, M., Durant, K. and Samuel, E. (2005) 'A systematic review of the impact of citizenship education on the learning and achievement', in *Research Evidence in Education Library.* London: Evidence for Policy and Practice Information and Co-ordinating Centre, Social Science Research Unit, Institute of Education.

Deakin Crick, R., McCombs B. *et al.* (2006) 'The ecology of learning: factors contributing to learner-centred classroom cultures', *Research Papers in Education* (forthcoming).

De Bono, E. (1985) *Six Thinking Hats.* Boston, MA: Little, Brown.

Fisher, R. (1995) *Teaching Children to Learn.* Cheltenham: Stanley Thornes.

Fisher, R. (2003) *Games for Thinking.* York: York Publishing Services.

Flutter, J. and Ruddick, J. (2004) *Consulting Pupils: What's in It for Schools?* London: Routledge Falmer.

Harlen, W. and Deakin Crick, R. (2003a) 'A systematic review of the impact of summative assessment and testing on pupils' motivation for learning', in *Research Evidence in Education Library.* London: Evidence for Policy and Practice Information and Co-ordinating Centre, Department for Education and Skills.

Harlen, W. and Deakin Crick, R. (2003b) 'Testing and Motivation for Learning', *Assessment for Education*, 10 (2), 169–208.

Infed (2005) Informal Education and Lifelong Learning website: **http://www.infed.org** (accessed April 2006).

James, L. (2002) *Opening Minds Project Update*. London: RSA.

Lakoff, G. and Johnson, M. (1980) *Metaphors We Live By*. Chicago, IL: University of Chicago Press.

McCombs, B. and Whisler, J. S. (1997) *The Learner Centered Classroom and School: Strategies for Increasing Student Motivation and Achievement*. San Francisco, CA: Jossey Bass.

McGettrick, B. (2002) 'Transforming School Ethos: Transforming Learning Citizenship Education in Action'. Paper presented at Bristol University Graduate School of Education.

Murris, K. and Haynes, J. (2000) *Storywise: Thinking Through Stories*. Newport: Dialogue Works.

RSA (2005) *Opening Minds: Giving Young People a Better Chance:* London: Royal Society for the encouragement of Arts, Manufactures & Commerce.

Sergiovanni, T. (1983) *Moral Leadership: Getting to the Heart of School Improvement*. San Francisco, CA: Jossey Bass.

Sergiovanni, T. (1994) 'Organisations or Communities? Changing the Metaphor Changes the Theory', *Educational Administration Quarterly*, 30 (2), 214–26.

Sergiovanni, T. (2000) *The Lifeworld of Leadership: Creating Culture, Community and Personal Meaning in Our Schools*. San Francisco, CA: Jossey Bass.

Small, T. (2004) *Developing Citizenship in Schools: Implications for Teachers and Students Arising from the EPPI Review of the Impact of Citizenship Education on the Provision of Schooling*. Bristol: Citizenship Education Review Group.

Staricoff, M. and Rees, A. (2003a) 'Thinking Skills Transform Our Days', *Teaching Thinking and Creativity*, 10, 40–3.

Staricoff, M. and Rees, A. (2003b) 'Start the Day on a Thought', *Teaching Thinking and Creativity*, 12, 40–4.

Staricoff, M. and Rees, A. (2004) 'The Four Fours Challenge', *Teaching Thinking and Creativity*, 15, 10–14.

Staricoff, M. and Rees, A. (2005) *Start Thinking*. Birmingham: Imaginative Minds Publishers.

Sutcliffe, R. and Williams, S. (2000) *The Philosophy Club: An Adventure in Thinking*. Newport: Dialogue Works.

Tew, M., Deakin Crick, R., Broadfoot, P. and Claxton, G. (2004) *Learning Power: A Practitioner's Guide*. Manchester: Lifelong Learning Foundation.

Wright, A. (1998) *Spiritual Pedagogy: A Survey, Critique and Reconstruction of Contemporary Spiritual Education in England and Wales*. Abingdon: Culham College Institute.

Index

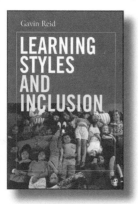